Updated: Using Clusters and Strategic Alliances along with Organizational Culture to Sustain Competitive Advantage

Dr. Spencer Hsieh

This study's model can assist corporations to create value-chain through improving activities, discover a new market space for a breakthrough in competitions.

Copyright © 2018 Spencer Hsieh

All rights reserved.

DESCRIPTION

The life cycle of organizations is getting shorter. If an organization is to maintain its competitive advantage it should not adhere to a concept of organizational life cycle in which an organization falls into the inevitable cycle of germination, growth, maturity, and death. Previous research on organizational change mostly emphasizes managing change, strategic change, specific interventions, or approaches to change that lead to organizational failure due to lack of innovation. Innovation can be in the form of a new product, a new service, or new technology. Any change should be based on a corporation's strategy, vision, values, and a corporation should promote an environment which supports and encourages such change.

By examining the impact that clusters and strategic alliances have upon a corporation's competitive advantage, this study aims to modify the existing organizational change model and provide guidance that corporations can use to maintain their competitive advantage. This study highlights that the optimum time for organizational change is during the growth period. The current research applies the concepts of organizational culture, cluster theory, and strategic alliance to the organizational change model. The output goals, a new product, a new way of operations, a new strategy, and a new culture, come from the organizational change process innovations.

The research obtained from this study has seven implications for management that have greatly contributed to a corporations' transition towards furthering their competitive advantage. When corporations come across difficult situations, the organizational change model can help corporations mitigate risk through the loop system. This study emphasizes an organization's entrepreneurial spirit due to easily influencing corporation's decision to initiate change that needs to adopt strategic alliances and clusters to connect with external environments in order to obtain new information and technology to maintain their competitiveness. However, Internet or the automobile can also has an impact on culture. Corporations must adjust their organizational culture to adapt to external change as well. In addition, this study's model can also assist corporations to create value-chain through improving activities, discover a new market space for a breakthrough in competitions, maintain long-term growth by continuously creating the second curve, and provide ISO 9000 and ISO 14000 standard functions.

CONTENTS

A	ACKNOWLEDGMENTS	i
B	ABOUT THE AUTHOR	101
1	Chapter1: Introduction	10

    1.1 Research questions and purposes

    1.2 Relevance to the field of management

2	Chapter 2: Literature Review & Research Proposition	17

    2.1 Organizational Transition

    2.2 Strategic Alliance and Cluster Theory

    2.3 Successful Clusters and Problems

3	Chapter 3: Research Framework	40

    3.1 Conceptual Model thinking route

    3.2 The development of organizational culture

    3.3 The development of strategic alliances

    3.4 The development of a cluster

    3.5 The development of organizational characteristics

3.6 Output goals

4 Chapter 4: Critical Evaluation 53

4.1 Method of Critical Evaluation

4.2 Results of Critical Evaluation

5 Chapter 5: Implications 59

5.1 Implications for management

5.2 Limitations and Future implications for research

6 *Appendix: 70

a. The expert reviewers

b. Evaluation Form

c. Integrated Evaluation Form

7 **B. Endnote** 87

8 **C. Reference** 88

D. List of Figures

Figure 2.1: The four organizational hurdles to strategy execution   18

Figure 2.2: The Transition Curve   19

Figure 2.3: Positive and Negative organization's entrepreneurial culture   22

Figure 2.4: The Second Curve — 24

Figure 2.5: The improvisational change model — 27

Figure 3.1: System Thinking : From Issues to Actions — 40

Figure 3.2: Conceptual framework of organizational change — 43

Figure 3.3: The organizational change model — 47

E. List of Tables

Table 1.1: Outlining all the approaches on change — 13

Table 2.1: Comparing the Curves — 25

Table 2.2: Organizational design strategies — 30

Table 2.3: Four types of clusters — 34

Table 3.1: The type of organizational integrating mechanism — 48

Table 3.2: Organizational change strategies — 50

Table 3.3: Output indicator's definition — 51

Table 4.1: Comments and Responses Form — 56

Table 5.1: Relevance to the contribution of management — 61

Spencer Hsieh

ACKNOWLEDGMENTS

For his assistance in bringing this book to market, I would like to thank Self-Publishing College, Johnny. Johnny has been my guide to the virtual world of book publishing. Truth be told, I initially found the prospect of writing a book to be an unnerving thing. However, with Johnny's ardent assistance, I was confident to pursue the dream of writing.

I am able to complete this strategy management' book also thanks University of Maryland University College Professor Booth and Professor Jim who gave me a valuable advice.

Professor Booth often told me that completing a good book required constantly reading and thinking in order to have your own ideas. This is really a sharp point.

Finally, I would also like to thank my wife for giving me the sincerest encouragement and support during my writing. My wife often told me that learning from mistakes could find the right answer from the mistakes.

I will only present this book to those who need constantly innovation and change.

CHAPTER1: INTRODUCTION

1.1 Research questions and purpose

An organization that does not adapt change cannot survive for long. Change is an essential feature of organizations life cycle. Previous research on organizational change mostly focuses on the structural contingency theory (Jokipii, 2010), political theory (Wines, 2008), organizational ecology theory (Zhou & Li, 2008), and institutional theory (Bruton, Ahlstrom, Li, 2010). These theories all emphasize the environmental changes that lead to organizational failure that is due to a lack of innovation (Ettlie, 1992; Hage, 1999). Innovation can take the form of a new product, a new service, new technology, a new process, or new administrative practices (Collins, Hage, & Hull, 1988; Ettlieetal, 1984; Ettlie, 1992). While theories of organizational change tend to focus on managing change, strategic change, specific interventions, or approaches to change (Whelan-Berry & Gordon, 2000), new competition in the market place or new demands by customers also stimulate or affect such changes. Such changes come about in response to the internal call for reform or in response to market failure, and are expected to bring forth improved efficiency, better service, or innovative products. However, an organizational change always encounters various obstacles and varying degrees of resistance. Changing an organization's values is better than changing strategies, structure, technologies, and products (Porter & Parker, 1992), so managers should strive to make flexibility an integral part of the values and norms of the organization in order to create a work environment that is open to change (Pasmore, 1994; Porter & Parker, 1992; Neal, 2009). Furthermore, corporate executives need to organize workshops and establish an employee committee by making full use of the integration of leadership, cross-cooperation, and technology (Neal, 2009; West, 2004; Yeo, 2009).

The life cycle of organizations is decreasing. If an

organization is to stay competitive, it should not adhere to a concept of the organizational life cycle in which an organization is born, grows old, and finally dies (Miller & Friesen, 1984; Churchill & Lewis, 1983; Mintzberg & Westley, 1992; Pietersen, 2002). In order to achieve competitive advantage, how can an organization create a new growth curve to enhance its competitive advantage? A corporation should undertake organizational change in its prime, rather than when the business is beginning to show signs of failure. Therefore, corporations must launch strategies to sustain development before they begin to lose momentum (Pietersen, 2002). This strategy is so-called a second curve. In order to achieve the second curve, the culture of the corporation and its characteristics must change alongside strategy. Once a corporation changes its strategy, it must realign its organizational culture with the new strategy. This is necessary because organizational culture and strategy are strongly interrelated. In addition, why do organizational design characteristics follow strategy change? Organizational strategy change signifies that organizational design characteristics are along with organizational goal change for maintenance competitiveness; otherwise, a corporation's strategy is likely to fail (Treacy & Wiersema, 1995; Higgins & Mcallaster, 2002; Daft, 2007). Any change should be based on a corporation's strategy, vision, and values. Additionally a corporation should create an environment that supports and promotes such change (Neal, 2009). Even in the process of reform, all actions taken in the name of change should be well managed in order to keep the organization moving towards its new vision and its stated objectives.

    This study focuses on how cluster theory and strategic alliances can be used to bring about organizational change. What is the relationship between corporations, clusters, and their strategic alliance? Clusters are geographically close groups of interconnected corporations and associated institutions in a particular field, which are linked by common technologies and skills (Porter, 1998, 2001). Clusters include

" governmental and other types of institutions such as universities, agencies of standardization, think tanks, and suppliers of specialized instruction, education, information, research and technical support" (Enache, Vechiu, & Morozan, 2009, p.38). A strategic alliance combines the information and insights of an alliance network with those of interfirm networks, thereby producing an important cross-level viewpoint of interorganizational relationships (Gulati, 1998). How can intercluster corporations or strategic alliances maintain competitive advantage? Corporation can share information, create new ways, and jointly solve problems through intercluster and strategic alliances with the aim of maintaining competitive advantage. However, both strategies are not panacea for staying competitive. What are the problems and risks? When a market changes too quickly and a product's life cycle is too short, it becomes more complicated for corporations to predict situations. Although clusters and strategic alliances also have drawbacks, the purpose of this study is to explore how cluster theory and strategic alliances can be used to promote organizational change through information sharing, technology spillover, and innovation.

How can an organization quickly identify and handle changes in the external environment? There are many approaches to facilitating organizational change, including the improvisational change model (Orlikowski & Hofman, 1997), TQM (Chong, Ooi, Lin and Teh, 2010), benchmarking learning (Grace & Hadyn, 2004), ISO quality management (Bonham, 2003), organizational restructuring (Barkema, 2008), business process reengineering (Chamberlin, 2010), as well as the linkage approach (Goodman and Rousseau, 2004). Among these organizational change approaches, the improvisational change model (Orlikowski & Hofman, 1997) is relatively reliable in terms of coping with cultural change, turbulent conditions within an organization, and new demands from an ever-changing market. The improvisational change model is typically a continuous process that requires explicit and persistent examination and adjustment along with the authority, credibility, influence, and resources needed to complete the organizational change. The improvisational change model includes three different types of sequential change: anticipated change, emergent change, and opportunity-based change. Leaders need to initiate organizational changes that allow employees to anticipate the changes that will be made to the organization and its culture. Subsequently, by developing a common view, a corporation increases communication among its employees, which in turn increases the likelihood of the employees accepting the corporation's policy. This is known as emergent change. Finally, owing to identification of the policy, leaders can identify the optimal opportunities needed to accomplish organizational change. These opportunities make up the competitive strategies of strategic alliance and cluster theory. This is the 'so-called opportunity-based change'. This research adds both aspects of the cluster theory and strategic alliances of the improvisational change model to the organizational change model, since this will help organizations to implement successful transitions and achieve their organizational goals. In addition, in order to compare above organizational change approaches with the improvisational change model, this study outlines all the approaches on change at the table 1.1.

Table 1.1: Outlining all the approaches on change

The approaches on change	The main of argument
TQM	TQM is a set of management practices throughout the organization, geared to ensure the organization consistently meets or exceeds customer requirements. TQM places strong focus on process measurement and controls as means of continuous improvement.

Benchmarking learning	The benchmarking learning provides a set of conceptually-derived criteria by which to compare the learning and development strategic focus of different organizations.
ISO quality management	The ISO concept is applicable to most every technical field (for example, ISO 9000 family for quality management and the ISO 14000 for environmental management systems) and provides a standards roadmap for virtually any type of corporation or product--from information technology to photography.
Organizational restructuring	Organizational performance ultimately rests on human behavior and improving performance requires changing behavior. Therefore, organizational restructuring should have as a fundamental goal the facilitation of clear, open communication that can enable organizational learning and clarify accountability for results.
Business process reengineering	Business process reengineering is the analysis and redesign of workflows and processes within an organization. Sometimes radical redesign and reorganization of an enterprise (wiping the slate clean) was necessary to lower costs and increase quality of service and that information technology was the key enabler for that radical change.
The linkage	Changes that successfully

| approach | improve performance in one part of the corporation often fail to translate into gains in firm-level performance. |

1.2 Relevance to the field of management

This study is relevant to the field of management since it covers organizational change, the improvisational change model, strategic alliances, and cluster theory. This will be illustrated in the next segment.

(1) Organizational change: Environmental change such as deregulation, privatization, technological change, or change in customer preferences stimulates organizational change. Organizational change always encounters many obstacles and various degrees of resistance. It is essential that organizational leaders create workshops and establish employee committees to impart the corporation's vision, which will only be realized through an integration of leadership, cross-cooperation, and technology (Suarez & Oliva, 2005; Neal, 2009; West, 2004; Yeo, 2009).

(2) The improvisational change model: The improvisational change model consists of three different types of change: anticipated change, emergent change, and opportunity-based change. The changes associated with technology constitute an ongoing process rather than an event with an end point after which the organization can expect to return to a reasonably steady state. In addition, all the technological and organizational changes are made during the ongoing process (Orlikowski & Hofman, 1997).

(3). Strategic alliance: This strategic alliance is a network, put emphasis on vertical relationships, lateral, and horizontal relationships among independent entities, as opposed to the so-called dyadic level. Strategic alliances can combine information and insights within the alliance network with intercorporation networks, and produce an important cross-level viewpoint of interorganizational relationships (Gulati, 1998; Farina Zylbersztain, 2003).

(4) Cluster theory: Clusters are geographically close groups of

interconnected companies and associated institutions within a particular field that are linked by common technologies and skills or use all forms of differentiating knowledge considered both key resources and key products (Porter, 1998, 2001; Enach, Vechiu & Morozan, 2009).

CHAPTER 2: LITERATURE REVIEW & RESEARCH PROPOSITION

2.1 Organizational Transition

Suarez & Oliva (2005) state that environmental changes such as deregulation, privatization, technological change, or changes in customer preferences (Kraats and Zajac, 2001) all stimulate organizational change. Moreover, environmental changes affect an organization's performance, lifespan, and development. These changes can be technological, economical, physical, social, or political. Clearly, environmental variation is a key factor when dealing with a range of issues and processes; including corporation survival, competitiveness, innovation, and executive turnover (Andrews, 1971; Christensen, 1992; Utterback & Suareze, 1993). Therefore, an organizational transition to success is ridden with much hardship caused by unexpected and unavoidable setbacks and failures.

Nelson and Winter (1982) state that organizations use routines that are developed through time and change constantly to adapt to changing conditions. This process of adaptation is referred to as organizational learning, optimally realized through proactive strategic planning (Weigl, Hartmann, Jahns & Darkow, 2008). When we regard organizational change as a strategy that adapts to external environment change, we adopt it as a deliberate decision-making strategy that aims to achieve or enhance organizational competitive advantage (Frahm, 2007).

In addition, not all organizational changes are driven by positive motivations such as achieving competitive advantage or making improvements to the workplace. In fact, most are the result of efforts to prolong the organization's development or to boost the waning momentum of business growth (Pietersen, 2002). Organizational changes usually face many difficulties. Mangers have assured us that the challenge is extremely difficult. They must face four hurdles. The first hurdle is cognitive that an organization wedded to the status quo; the second hurdle is limited resources; the third difficulty is unmotivated staff; the final obstacle is politics that opposition from powerful vested interests (See Figure 2.1) (Kim & Mauborgne, 2005). However, few corporation managers face these hurdles that can break from status quo. For example, 75%-83% of organizations fail to achieve their objectives (Andersen, Buvik, & Torvatn, 2007). Even "Jack Welch needed some ten years and tens of millions of dollars of restructuring and training to turn GE into a powerhouse" (Kim & Mauborgne, 2005, p. 149).

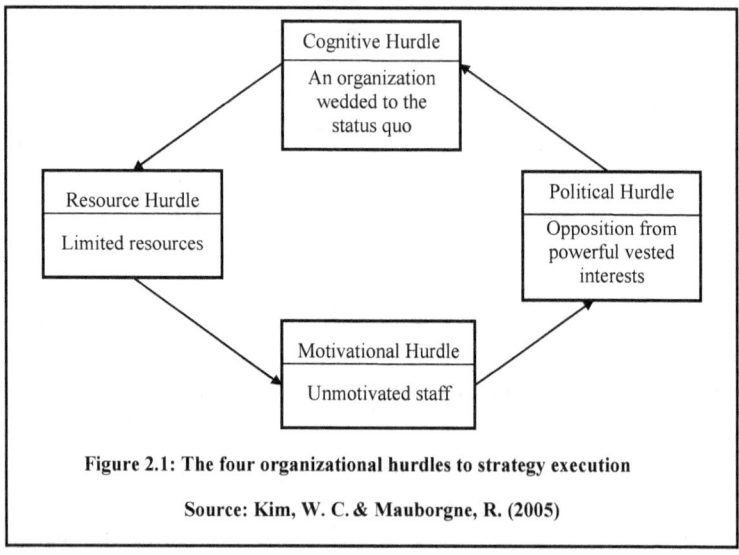

Figure 2.1: The four organizational hurdles to strategy execution

Source: Kim, W. C. & Mauborgne, R. (2005)

Thus, it is important for leaders to help employees go through the natural phases of the transition curve, from denial to commitment (Neal, 2009) (See Figure 2.2), because organizational change may induce uncertainty and cause resistance (Andersen, et al, 2007). Therefore, the leaders who adapt to managing changes are those who convert resistance into support by understanding and following the six golden rules for successful change: creating a simple obliging statement of the case for change, communicating often and honestly throughout the process, maximizing participation, removing those who resist, generating short-term wins, and setting up a shining example (Pietersen, 2002). However, in order to convert resistance into support, an empirical investigation of ethical leadership found that ethical leadership plays a mediating role in connecting with employee willingness to put in extra effort, employee satisfaction with the leader, and transformational culture (Toor & Ofori, 2009). Based on the above research, the study presents the following research proposition.

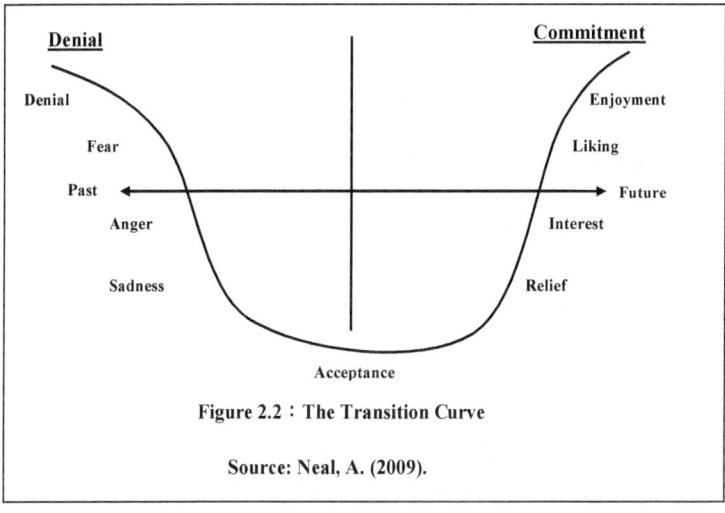

Figure 2.2 : The Transition Curve

Source: Neal, A. (2009).

Proposition1: Organizational transition is initiated by deregulation, privatization, technological change, and changes in customer preferences. These external change factors impact organizational survival, competitiveness, innovation, and executive turnover.

Proposition2: Organizational changes usually are met with difficulties such as employees' resistance; therefore, leaders must convert resistance into support through communication, maximizing participation, and transformational culture.

In addition to the above proposition, successful change also requires an understanding of cultural change, change in successful stages, as well as the process of change.

2.1.1 Cultural change

Changes in the external environment entail changes in technology, strategy, structure, and corporate cultural values and norms. Many corporations fail to accomplish their goals because of ignorance of cultural factors (Prajogo & McDermott, 2005). Moreover, organizational change can be successful only when employees are willing to devote their time and energy to reach new goals and are able to endure the resulting stress and hardship. Clearly communicating a vision that embodies flexibility and openness to new ideas, methods, and styles will set the stage for a change-oriented organization to help employees cope with the chaos and tension associated with change (Recardo, Molloy & Pellegrino, 1995/1996). Some primary changes require a shift both in organizational culture and employee mindset, and can thus help the organization move towards horizontal forms of organizing, greater employee and customer diversity, and a shift in the way an organization learns (Daft, 2007). Hence, organizational culture develops as the organization "learns to deal with its problems of external adoption and internal integration" (Schein, 1985, p5) and the predominant role of human (interorganization) interaction (Eisenberg & Riley, 2000; Dixon, 2010). Organizational culture is, "Where the purpose is development of an imaginary, aspired, and desirable organizational culture...it is a symbolic management which has its objective to create an exceptional and specific culture" (Kuchinsakas & Paulauskaite, 2005, p.147). It includes the confidence that organizational culture can be created and can result in a positive outcome for an organization.

An organization's culture generally begins with a founder or early leader who articulates and implements particular ideas and values as a vision, philosophy, or business strategy. When these ideas and values lead to success, they become institutionalized, and an organizational culture emerges that reflects the vision and strategy of the founder or leader. In addition, as corporations have to deal with rapid and discontinuous change from the external environment, it has been suggested that organizations need to become more entrepreneurial (Hitt, 2000). An entrepreneurial culture is " one in which new ideas and creativity are expected, risk-taking is encouraged, failure is tolerated, learning is promoted, product, process, and administrative innovations are championed, and continuous change is viewed as a conveyer of opportunities" (Ireland, Hitt & Sirmon, 2003, p.970). Such an entrepreneurial culture will cause a positive relationship between a manager's mindset and an organizational culture that will build an organizational spiral that will bring about employees centripetal force (identify organization's policy), and feedback loops between bottom-up and top-down which continues to be a permanent relationship (Shepherd, Patzelt & Haynie, 2010). Conversely, if an organization presents a decreasing spiral, employees will lack centripetal force (See Figure 2.3). Hence, in order to keep a positive entrepreneurial culture, the manager must increasingly be aware that an entrepreneurial mindset impacts upon organizational employees. For example, if a manager with an increasingly entrepreneurial mindset is prepared to communicate and act upon this new knowledge, those actions may result in knowledge spillover from the manager to organizational employees. In that case, organizational employees will also perceive entrepreneurial action as more feasible, and thus the new-shared knowledge will impact the organization's culture.

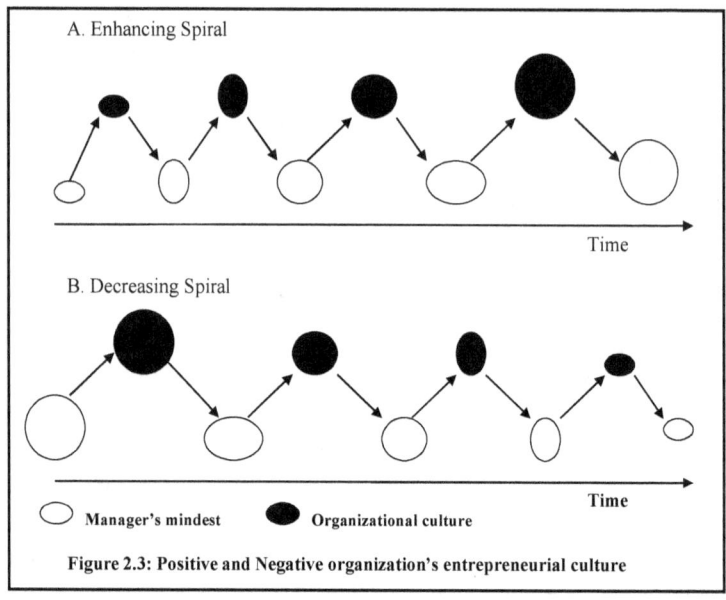

Figure 2.3: Positive and Negative organization's entrepreneurial culture

Source: Shepherd, D. A., Patzelt, H., & Haynie, J. M. (2010).

When adapting to changing situations within dynamic environments, the make-up of an organizations cultural change becomes ever more important. "Cultural change" refers to changes in the values, attitudes, expectations, beliefs, abilities, and behavior of the members of an organization. Cultural change also pertains to changes in how employees think; these are changes in mindset rather than technology, structure, or products (Schein, 1992; Kotter & Heskett, 1992).

Organizational culture helps to guide the daily activities of workers in meeting certain goals, because it helps members adapt to the external environment. Organizational culture also helps the organization rapidly respond to customers' needs or the moves of a competitor (Daft, 2007). Although culture can bring numerous benefits to an organization, it needs to be geared towards meeting particular goals. Organizational development (OD) can help diversify cultural change (Allen & Montgomery, 2001). This is because OD emphasizes the values of human development, fairness, openness, freedom from coercion, and individual autonomy, all of which allow workers to perform the job as they see fit, within reasonable organizational constraints (Warner Burke, 2000). The above discussion can be summarized in the form of the following research proposition.

Proposition 3: Corporations fail to accomplish their goals on account of ignorance of cultural factors because an organization's culture can help the organization to rapidly respond to external environment's rapid and discontinuous dynamism.

2.1.2 Implementing change while in the successful stage

Organizational change, if well managed, can avoid falling into the inevitable cycle of germination, growth, maturity, and death (Mintzberg & Westley, 1992), which is what is referred to as the "first curve." Organizational change is best conducted when the corporation is currently within a successful period. Therefore, corporations should not start their organizational change when they are on the verge of going of business or showing signs of failure. As shown in figure 2.4, the best time for organizational change is point A for maintaining competitive advantage. This change created the second curve at point A. The shaded area shows the critical time for implementing organizational change. On the contrary, the worst time for implementing change is when an organization has already begun to decline (point B) (Pietersen, 2002).

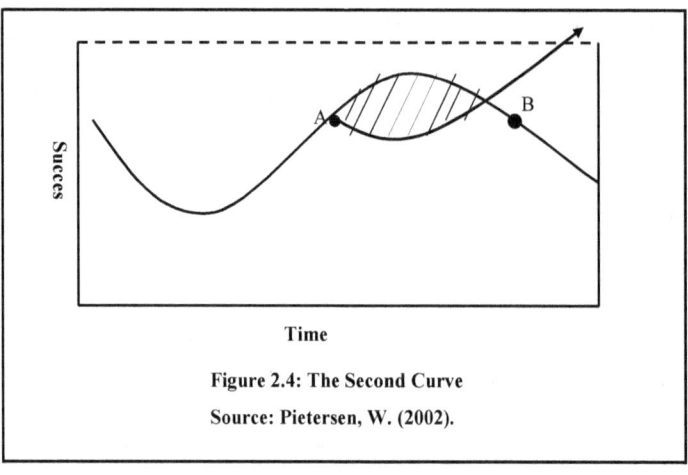

Figure 2.4: The Second Curve
Source: Pietersen, W. (2002).

How can we tell when we are at the end of the first curve and entering the second ? The signs are revenue growth will flatten and even decline slighted (Morrison, 1998; Andrus, 2004). For example, Microsoft does not shift from the first curve (the Windows platform) to the second cure (the Internet) until the Windows platform's revenue has declined. The Apple computer company began conducting research for its iPhone 4G shortly after its iPhone 3G began to be met with substantial demand that resulted in a high level of sales. Both Microsoft and Apple have successfully altered their strategy (the first curve) and prepared for the second curve while they are in their prime. In addition, Microsoft and Apple are both cases in which successful change created the second curve so as to maintain competitive advantage.

The first curve is that a corporation's traditional business carried out in a familiar corporate climate. The second curve is the future of new technologies, new consumers, and new markets that will combine to bring about an overall and unalterable alteration in the way every business must organize and function (Pouzar, 1996; Morrison, 1998; Andrus, 2004). When comparing alternate ways between the first curve and the second curve, Morrison (1998) theorized that the first curve focused on capital, computer, horizontal and vertical integration, business processes, and hard work, whereas the second curve focused on the knowledge, Internet, virtual integration, culture, and hyper-effectiveness. Morrison further compared the first curve with the second curve according to market, organization, and individual (See Table 2.1).

In addition, implications of the second curve for organizations can be observed a number of different organizations of the future. What types of organizations are located within the second curve organization? These organizations are not intended to be prescriptive, but descriptive such as the hyper-focused corporation, the cultural juggernaut, the extended enterprise, the shared-risk alliance, the fishnet organization, and the chaotic enterprise (Morrison, 1998). The hyper-focused corporation is like a Silicon Valley startup or a corporation division with a single mission, involving turned-on people who work all night until the early hours of the morning. The cultural juggernaut organization runs on the basis of values like Amway, Volvo.

The extended corporation is a vertically integrated corporation that looks for development and seeks to maintain long-term relationships with suppliers and distributors. The shared-risk alliance enterprises share competences for mutual benefits through networks and alliances. The fishnet enterprise is a web of continual changing hierarchies connected and managed through information technology. The chaotic enterprise is like Visa that combines chaos and order (Morrison, 1998).

Table 2.1 Comparing the Curves

The first curve market focuses on:	The second curve market focuses on :
Capital *	* Knowledge
Producer *	* Consumer

The Atlantic ∗	∗ The Pacific
Japan ∗	∗ China
International Trade ∗	∗ Electronic commerce
Computers ∗	∗ Internet
Money ∗	∗ people
The first curve organization focuses on:	The second curve organization focuses on:
Engineering ∗	∗ Ecology
Corporations ∗	∗ Individuals and networks
Horizontal and vertical integration ∗	∗ Virtual integration
	∗ Culture
Business processes ∗	
The first curve individual focuses on:	The second curve individual focuses on:
Hard work ∗	∗ Hyper-effectiveness
Security ∗	∗ Uncertainty
Current career ∗	∗ Future career
Faith ∗	∗ Hope
Loyalty ∗	∗ Courage

Sources: Morrison, J, I. (1998).

How does an organization seize this optimal opportunity

(point A)? An organization's leader often overestimates the impact a phenomenon will have in the short term, and underestimates the impact it will have in the long run. Hence, a corporation cannot precisely predict how it will be affected by such external factors including the development of new technology, new consumer demands, and the emergence of new markets. Such forces create much uncertainty and unrest within a corporation. Phillips asserts, "When an entire business is at the end of the value stability stage and near the cusp of the beginnings of value outflow it is time for a leadership change" (2010, p25). And, "There is no standard model of how a company should respond to a decline in its profitability and market position" (2010, p25).

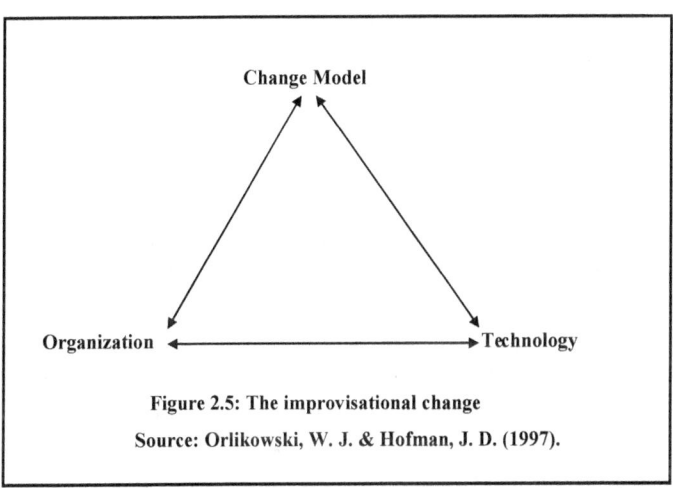

Figure 2.5: The improvisational change
Source: Orlikowski, W. J. & Hofman, J. D. (1997).

The current study supports Phillips viewpoint. As there is no standard model, this study tries to use the improvisational change model (See Figure 2.5) to help corporations to complete a successful organizational transition by resolving these impacts through such competitive strategies as strategic alliance and clustering. Based on above research, this study presents the following research proposition.

Proposition 4: In order to gain a competitive advantage, organizational change should take place while the organization is in its prime, rather than when it begins to fail or decline.

2.1.3 Change Process

In effect, the improvisational change model needs to go through anticipated, emergent, and opportunity-based organizational changes over time. Anticipated change completes its intended aim by facilitating communication among members of the organization. Emergent change arises spontaneously from local innovation. Opportunity-based change is not anticipated, but introduced purposefully (Orlikowski & Hofman, 1997). In addition, the change process must be aligned with the change model (to manage change), the technology, and the organization (including culture, structure, roles, and responsibilities). Every change process relies on the interaction among these three dimensions that provide continuous support for the process of change. This improvisational change model is typically a continuous process that requires explicit and persistent examination and adjustment, along with the authority, credibility, influence, and resources needed to complete the organizational change (Orlikowski & Hofman, 1997). Therefore, an organization (a clustered corporation) in its prime increases its competitive advantage and competitor awareness. When the clustered corporations are in the decline phase, they begin to experience wasted resources, isolated competitive practices, less innovation, and eventually they lose dominance in the industry (Pouder & ST. John, 1996). Therefore, when a corporation is still in the successful phase, if it fails to adopt the improvisational change model for maintaining its competitive advantage, it is predestined to decline.

In summary, when an organization faces external changes, such as new production technology, changes in costs, and new demands, it needs to create the second curve in order to maintain its competitive advantage. An organization needs to continually formulate new strategies in response to environmental changes. The second curve shows how an organization successfully responds to environmental change, and focuses on ecology, individuals and networks, virtual integration, and culture (Morrison, 1998). Owing to environmental change, organizational strategy follows change along with organization design characteristic. For example, the goal is to achieve the second curve; strategies are a plan for interacting with competitive environment to achieve the second curve. Organization wants to achieve the second curve that organization design characteristic must follow change because of strategies change; how the choice of strategic affects organization design. Organization design characteristics need to support the corporation's competitive strategies. For example, with a low-cost leadership strategy, corporation leaders take an efficiency approach to organizational design. A low-cost leadership connects with strong central authority, tight cost control, with frequent detailed control reports, standard operating procedures, and highly efficient procurement and distribution systems. Employees generally carry out routine tasks under close supervision (Porter, 1980). Table 2.2 compares Porter's competitive strategies with the strategy typology of Miles and Snow.

Based on the above viewpoints, this study adopts the competitive strategy of strategic alliances and cluster theory, an approach which can help organizations create platforms and opportunities for organizational success transition, as well as platforms for entering into industrial clusters, and creating interdependent cooperative sectors within geographic proximity (Gwee, 2009). For example, by using strategic alliances and the cluster strategy, the automotive steel clusters in Hamilton, the automotive parts clusters in Windsor, the aerospace clusters in Montreal, and the mining and services cluster in Sudbury can help traditional manufacturing and resource industries reduce the competitive pressure of the global market and engage in innovation and learning development*. (Warrian & Mulhern, 2009). This will be illustrated in the next segment.

Table 2.2: Organizational design strategies

Porter's Competitive Strategies	Miles and Snow's Strategy Typology
Strategy: Differentiation **Organizational Design:** • Learning orientation acts in a flexible, loosely knit way, with strong horizontal coordination • Strong capability in research • Values and builds in mechanisms for customer intimacy • Rewards employee creativity, risk taking, and innovation **Strategy:** Low-Cost Leadership **Organizational Design:** • Efficiency orientation; strong central authority, tight cost control, with frequent, detailed control reports	**Strategy:** Prospector **Organizational Design:** • Learning orientation; flexible, fluid, decentralized structure • Strong capability in research **Strategy:** Defender **Organization Design:** • Efficiency orientation; centralized authority and tight cost control • Emphasis on production efficiency; low overheads • Close supervision; little employee empowerment **Strategy:** Analyzer **Organizational Design:** • Balances efficiency and learning; tight cost control with flexibility and adaptability • Efficient production for stable product

• Standard operating procedures • Highly efficient procurement and distribution systems • Close supervision; routine tasks, limited employee empowerment	lines; emphasis on creativity, research, risk-taking for innovation **Strategy:** Reactor **Organizational Design:** • No clear organizational approach; design characteristics may shift abruptly, depending on current needs

Source: Porter, M. E, (1980).; Treacy, M. & Wiersema, F. (1995); Miles, R. E., Snow, C. C., Meyer, A. D. & Coleman, H.J. (1978).

2.2 Strategic Alliance and Clusters

Organizational change aimed at developing new production technology, realizing cost differences, and adapting to new demands involves three components: departmental specialization, boundary spanning, and horizontal coordination (Daft, 2007). These three components are closely related to the competitive strategy of strategic alliance and clusters. The key departments in new product development are R&D and corporation. Boundary spanning needs linkages with relevant sectors in the external environment. Horizontal coordination means that technical, marketing, and production staff share ideas and information. All three of these components need to be implemented for the strategic alliance and cluster approach to be effective.

2.2.1 Strategic Alliance

A strategic alliance is not a dyadic level, but a network which combines information and insight through interfirm networks, producing an important cross-level viewpoint of interorganizational relationships (Gulati, 1998). The concept of a network expands the chain concept by emphasizing not only vertical relationships, but also lateral and horizontal relationships among independent entities (Farina and Zylbersztain, 2003). Network collaboration is characterized by short- or medium-term relationships, which are often project-based, among members (Matopoulos, Vlachopoulou & Manthou, 2006). As Mukherjee emphasizes, "No company can do well if its network is failing" (2009, p24), indicating that strong interconnectedness and a high degree of capability complementarily among network partners are critical to a corporation's success (Weigl, Hartmann, Johns & Darkow, 2008). Moreover, a corporation's strategic alliances can form a cluster effect through inter-organizational learning and resource sharing (Gulati, 1999). Clustering is an embedded structure created by the dense ties between partners, and can be built on common products or services through universities, standards agencies, and trade associations. Corporations belonging to the cluster share information about trustworthiness, capabilities, and objectives. In addition, clustering can help create common languages and define, and solve problems (Cowan & Jonard, 2009). For example, DoCoMo is a traditional Japanese mobile telecommunications company that used networking to develop the technology for mobile video streaming over wired and wireless networks. The company formed strategic partnerships with Packet Videa, Fujitsu, Inc., and NMS Communications (in the USA) to develop video footage 3G mobile phones and PDAs (Kodama, 2005). The company operating income has also increased.

Although corporations can employ strategic alliances to network successfully and make use of the cluster effect, they must carefully monitor their partners, because not all strategic alliances for complementary technologies are beneficial (Hill, 1992). It is possible that an alliance partner will exploit an alliance by pirating knowledge while giving little in return. Besides, since a corporation's leader can watch and manage only a limited number of strategic alliances, the corporation's effectiveness will fall with the number of strategic alliances to which it is committed (Schilling & Hill, 1998). These risks can be mitigated by conducting a detailed search for potential partners before entering into an alliance. The strategic alliance of the potential partner requires the coordination of capabilities and relationships. This includes defining the roles and responsibilities of the internal participants and external components, developing a vision about the future, realizing the process, and managing change over time (Rainey, 2006).

2.2.2 Cluster theory

According to Enache, Vechiu & Morozan state, "A cluster means a network of corporations which use all forms of differentiating knowledge considered both key resources and key products. The focus lies on organizational learning which is at the basis of functioning statutes and regulations" (2009, p38). Porter defines clusters as "geographically close groups of interconnected companies and associated institutions in a particular field linked by common technologies and skills" (2001, p7). Clusters can increase a geographical area's competitiveness and thus enhance its rate of economic growth (Porter, 1998). Industrial clusters fall into four general types: Marshallian, hub-and-spoke, satellite platforms, and state-anchored (Markusen, 1996; Pickernell, Rowe, Christie & Brooks, 2007) (See Table 2.3). Marshallian clusters are formed by locally owned, small-and medium-size corporations in the information- and technology-intensive industries. Hub-and-spoke clusters are controlled by one or several large corporations surrounded by related input suppliers and service providers. Satellite platforms are made up of branches of large multi-plant companies that are headquartered outside the cluster. State-anchored clusters exist in regions where the local economy is dominated by a large public or non-profit organization, such as a research facility, a university, or a defense plant. In addition, regions and regionalization through business cluster has shrunk national boundaries, such as Europe and North America (Damson, 2009). Each of these clusters offers a different degree of interfirm interdependence and outlook for growth.

Table 2.3: Four types of clusters

Cluster Type	Characteristics of Member Corporations	Intracluster Interdependence	Job Growth outlook
Marshallian	Small and medium, locally owned corporations	Substantial interfirm trade and collaboration; strong institutional support	Relies on synergies, economies provided by cluster
Hub-and-spoke	One or several large corporations with numerous smaller suppliers and service corporations	Cooperation between large corporations and smaller suppliers, on the terms of the larger corporations	Relies on the growth outlook of large corporations
Satellite platform	Medium and large branch plants	Minimal intercorporation trade and networking	Relies on a region's ability to recruit and retain branch plants
State-anchored	Large public or non-profit entity and related	Restricted to buy-sell relationships between entities	Relies on region's ability to maintain

	supplying service corporation	and suppliers	political support for public facilities

Source: Pickernell, D., Rowe, P. A., Christie, M. J. & Brooksbank, D. (2007).

The cluster must be based on something unique that is difficult to imitate (Perry, 1999). It acts as a broker between sectors and individual interests with the aim of sustaining competitive advantage. As it is formed by different corporations becoming closely tied together in the form of an alliance, clustering is an embedded structure. Corporations belonging to the same cluster share information regarding trustworthiness, capabilities, and objectives. Therefore, alliance networks emerge as a dynamic process driven by exogenous interdependencies (Cowan & Jonard, 2009).

For this reason, when a corporation whose internal and relational capabilities are not transparent undertakes innovation, the corporation does not benefit from the complementary relationships that exist between internal and external resources. In order to prove the above assumption, Hervas-Oliver & Albors-Garrigos (2009) studied 48 small- and medium-size enterprises (SMEs) belonging to one of the leading European ceramic tile clusters. They find that a corporation's strategy needs to be understood as a combination of both internal and external relational resources that can influence innovation and partially shape the dynamics of a cluster.

The above discussion can be summarized in the form of the following research proposition.

Proposition5: Corporations in the intercluster can combine internal and external resources to enhance organizational competitiveness. Clusters and strategic alliances can be used to enhance organizational competitive strategies.

2.3 Successful Clusters and Problems
2.3.1 Successful Clusters

Successful clusters depend on their capacity to absorb, diffuse, and exploit the knowledge required from extra-cluster sources, as well as on the willingness of member corporations to play the role of gatekeeper. When the intra-cluster system is weakly interconnected and the degree of external openness is very limited, the members of the cluster do not have dense ties and do not form alliances to counter potential risks. Therefore, if the cluster has no links with extra-cluster sources, and none of the corporations in the cluster play the role of gatekeeper (Giuliani, 2009), then it is likely that risks will increase and problems will become more complex.

Clusters go beyond traditional vertical supply chains and horizontal networks, operating more as cross-sectional oral networks consisting of dissimilar and complementary corporations (Maskell, 2001). Corporations in the downstream industry locate where there are a large proportion of upstream corporations in order to save trading costs on their inputs. The combined result of these "demand pull" and "cost push" considerations are gathering in a mass of activity in a cluster (Athiyaman & Parkan, 2008). Clusters are regarded as encompassing an array of linked industries and other entities important to competition. They include suppliers of input components, machinery, services, and extend downstream to companies related by skills and technologies, as well as extending to customers. Hence, clusters allow an organization to centralize and shorten its supply chain (Dewitt, Giunipero & Melton, 2006). Clusters are geographic concentrations of interconnected companies and institutions in a particular field. They can increase the productivity of companies within a specific area, drive the direction and pace of innovation, and stimulate the formation of new businesses (Porter, 1998).

What is a successful cluster? Gupta & Subramanian (2008) identify four models of regional clustering and its competitive advantage: the scale model, the innovation model, the intermediation model, and the regulation model. Derived from local externalities, the scale model is oriented towards the generic strategy of overall cost leadership. The innovation model is oriented towards the generic strategy of differentiation, and is derived from the cluster's capacity to learn and improve based on deep cross-sectional oral linkages among sophisticated factors, customers, channels, and rivals. The intermediation model allows corporations to strengthen their connections within the cluster. The model is also used to discover and develop new connections outside of the cluster. The regulation model helps in making decisions about local vs. global connections to maintain the corporation's advantage. An organization in the successful cluster is able to make organizational changes successfully. Based on above research, the paper presents the following research proposition.

Proposition 6: A successful cluster can play the role of gatekeeper and connect well with extra-cluster resources that can centralize and shorten its supply chain.

Proposition 7: A corporation in the cluster can be oriented towards the generic strategy of overall cost leadership and differentiation, and strengthen local vs global connections to maintain corporation's advantage.

2.3.2 Problems and crises

Old organizations or clusters must find new methods that combine different fields with their external network to remake the cluster (Tseng & Shih, 2008); otherwise, the older cluster cannot sustain itself. In addition, clusters consisting of corporations with a weak knowledge base have a highly disconnected intra-cluster knowledge system and will have poor connection to the external world (Giuliani, 2009). Thus, it can be seen that if the cluster has no links with extra-cluster sources of knowledge and none of the corporations play the role of technological gatekeepers, the cluster will not bring any competitive advantage to the corporation.

Clearly, clusters are not a panacea for enhancing a corporation's competitiveness, because rapid market development and technological change make it more difficult for corporations to devise contingencies. This also leads to conflicts between partner corporations and thus impedes cooperation. Moreover, asymmetrical information sharing between corporations may also induce uncertainty regarding a potential partner's competencies and incentives (Lorenzen, 2002). All these problems affect the benefits gained by the cluster's members. Cluster policy should return to coordination mechanisms operating in institutional environments (Lorenzen, 2002), or else a cluster will become a collective entity that lacks competitiveness.

Among the various conditions of success for a cluster, trust is one of the most important. Corporations need to understand the importance of trust in industrial clusters and how it arises. Khan & Ghani (2004) identified the following risks regarding clusters:

(1) Incorrect regional policies, often designed to help distressed areas, often end up fragmenting scarce human and capital resources, thereby damaging cluster development (Pouder & St. John, 1996).

(2) When trust breaks down, unwritten rules must be encoded and third parties brought in to resolve differences. Furthermore, distrust increases harmful conflict, transaction costs, and the possibility of crisis and failure.

Due to the fact that clusters make use of common resources, the geographic character of a cluster tends to raise the "tragedy of the commons" issue (Matopoulos, Vlachopoulou & Manthou, 2006). This risk is especially high for strong clusters and needs further exploration. The greatest risks are related to highly automated or routine operations, such as those that are used to train a workforce, and may include high-paying jobs, because of the high productivity and criticality of the automated or routine operations. As these operations are outsourced, a significant hole is left within the local regional cluster, threatening its scale and scope (Gupta & Subramanian, 2008).

A further problem is the risk of aggregate failure. For example, in order to stimulate innovation in a regional cluster, governments or decision makers tend to attempt to imitate the success of famous high-tech regional clusters elsewhere, such as the Xinzhu Science Park (Taiwan), Silicon Valley (US), Bavaria (Germany), Sophia-Antipolis (France), and Oulu (Finland) (Hospers, 2005). As a result, all science parks around the globe are very much alike and usually include companies specializing in biotechnology, information and communications technology (ICT), multimedia, life sciences, and energy. Therefore, cluster policy runs the risk of overinvestment that results in overcapacity and cost reduction instead of innovation (Visser & Atzema, 2008). Jacobs and Lankhuizen (2006, p247) state, "Porter (1990, 1998, 2001) called upon governments to focus on particular and traditional competitive strengths, not to imitate the success of others." Porter's viewpoint, not to imitate the success of clusters, does not seem to be accurate because all science parks in the whole world are imitation each other. The above discussion can be summarized in the form of the following research proposition.

Proposition 8: Clusters are not a panacea for enhancing a corporation's competitiveness, because imitation, incorrect regional policy, distrust, and using the same open source are the cluster's main weaknesses.

CHAPTER 3: RESEARCH FRAMEWORK

3.1 Conceptual Model Thinking Route

Based on the above propositions, this study uses a system of thinking (Senge, 1994; Sterman, 2000; Gharajedaghi, 2007) to analyze organizational change and establish research framework. What are the most important issues for maintaining organizational competitive advantage? It is crucial that an organization adapts internally in order to respond to changes in the external environment. Which variables are increasing or decreasing? What are the most important trends or problem? What are the system forces for creating the change? Can we influence it? Finally, it is very important to have an understanding of strategy complete action plan. Figure 3.1 is the thought process I used.

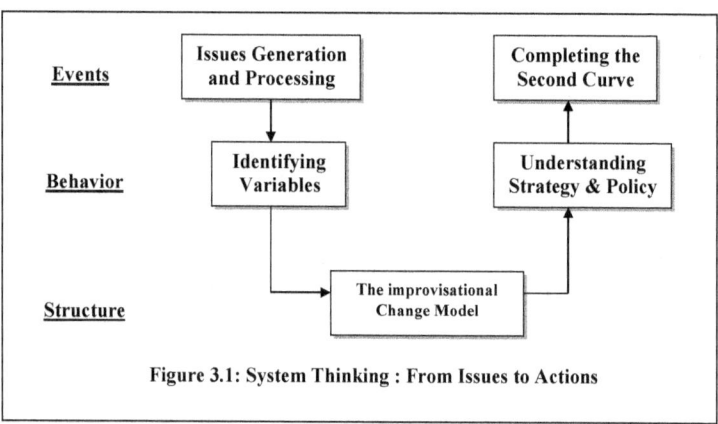

Figure 3.1: System Thinking : From Issues to Actions

The challenge is to maintain a corporation's competitive advantage. Due to dynamic change in external variables, such as new technology, customer preference, deregulation, the availability of better services, and innovative products, the corporation leaders must identify variable factors to corporation's diffusion range. Hence, this study shows that the improvisational change model, which is composed of an ongoing process rather than an event (Orlikowski & Hofman,

1997), is an appropriate way of reaching the stage where an organization can successfully implement change. The improvisational change model for managing organizational change is based on external environmental factors and the use of competitive strategic technology, strategic alliances and cluster theory. The improvisational change model includes three different types of change: anticipated, emergent, and opportunity-based. Anticipated change occurs when a corporation's leaders initiate change (the second curve) to achieve their intended goal in facilitating better communication among members of the organization. In emergent change, the intended goals (the second curve) are emphasized using informal communication throughout the corporation. This change is deemed necessary when the intended goal (the second curve) has become extinct and the corporation's leader must adapt corporate culture in response to changes in the external environment. In opportunity-based change, a corporation makes use of a competitive strategy, such as a strategic alliance or cluster. Both anticipated and opportunity-based change includes deliberate action, in contrast with emergent change, which appears spontaneously (Orlikowski, 1996).

The improvisational change model lies in the area between the first curve and the second curve. All current profit comes from the first curve, but future growth is determined by the second curve (Morrison, 1998). It takes time for the second curve to become established and the first curve to wane. Consequently, both curves need to coexist for some time. The problem is that if you jump from the first curve too soon, you will fail to lay the groundwork needed to build the second curve (Blanchard, 1996; Morrison, 1998). Hence, the shaded area (see figure 2.3) represents the critical time that the organization has to shift from the first curve to the second curve.

In developing the organizational change model, three important elements are introduced as the core competence:

culture, strategic alliance, and clustering. In the following, the conceptual framework of the organizational change model is first introduced. Following this, culture, strategic alliance, and cluster are defined. Finally, the reasons why they are necessary and how the three can function in the organizational change model is illustrated.

The conceptual framework of the organizational change model is shown in figure 3.2. In figure 3.2, the external environmental change factors are regarded as the trigger (input) of the change in an organization. The second curve is the outcome of organizational change or enhanced competitiveness, such as a new product, a new way of operating, a new strategy, or a new culture. To launch the second curve, an organization must cope with external factors through strategic alliances and participation in an industrial cluster. The improvisational change model adopted for coping with external factors involves "process." The strategic alliances and participation in an industrial cluster provides links to outside organizations.

Strategies affect organizational characteristics. When an organization adopts the improvisational change model and strategies (strategic alliance and clustering), the organization design characteristics need to support the corporation's competitive approach (Treacy & Wiersema, 1995). For example, if a corporation wants to change during the growth stage, it must become a second-curve organization that focuses on networks, the Internet, innovation, and integration.

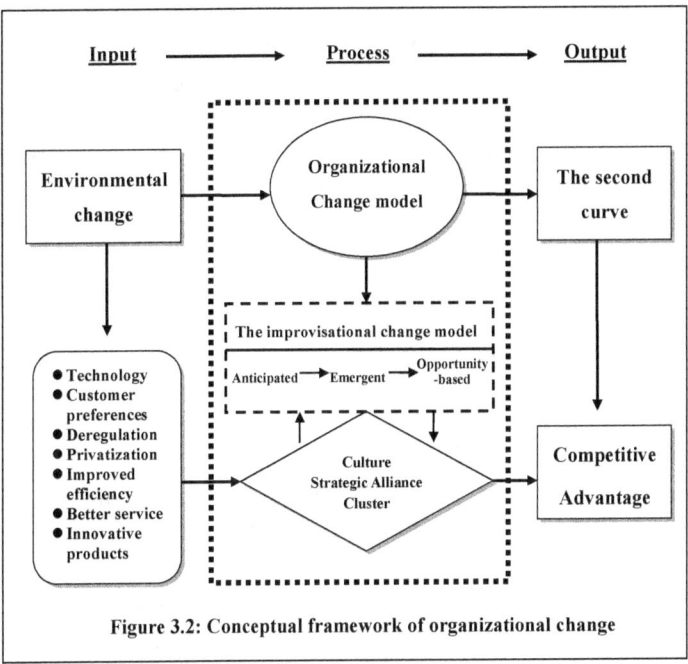

Figure 3.2: Conceptual framework of organizational change

The approach of this study is set out in figure 3.2. The "process" includes the development of organizational culture, the development of strategic alliances, the development of clusters, the improvisational change model, and the development of organizational characteristics (See Figure 3.3). The "output" includes new products, ways of operating, strategies, and culture. These are illustrated in the next section.

3.2 The development of organizational culture

Organizational culture is defined as a set of values, norms, guidelines, beliefs, and understandings that are shared by members of an organization. A beneficial organizational culture emphasizes openness, collaboration, teamwork, innovation, and constant change (Brown & Starkey, 1994; Schein, 1990; Higgins & McAllaster, 2002). When a corporation undertakes organizational change, it should emphasize both strategy and structural design. If the external environment requires flexibility and responsiveness, the culture should encourage adaptability. An understanding of the relationship between cultural values, organizational strategy and structure, and the environment can enhance organizational competitiveness (Chatman & Cha, 2003; Ghobadian & O'Regan, 2002). Therefore, a corporation should strive to align its culture with its current strategy. When adopting this method, employees can understand clearly what the corporation expects of them.

Organizational culture can be assessed along a number of different dimensions, two of which are focused on in this study: adaptability culture and clan culture (Denison & Mishra, 1995). The success of these two dimensions depends on the needs of the external environment and the organization's strategic focus, such as strategic alliance and cluster theory. The adaptability culture focuses on flexibility, creativity, innovation, and entrepreneurship towards the external environment. It encourages entrepreneurial values, norms, and beliefs that support the capacity of the organization in detecting, interpreting, and translating signals from the environment into new behavior. The clan culture focuses on participation, teamwork, and commitment towards the internal environment. It also focuses on adapting to rapidly changing expectations from the external environment. In a clan culture, an important value is taking care of employees and making sure they have access to resources needed to perform their job roles so that they will be satisfied and productive (Cameron & Freeman, 1991; Hooijberg & Petrock, 1993; McDermott & Stock, 1999; Zu, Robbins & Fredendall, 2010).

Therefore, organizational culture can integrate internal employees' different opinions and adapt external outsiders' change, and then help workers to meet the company goals.

3.3 The development of strategic alliances

The development of strategic alliances is defined as a competitive strategy that pushes an organization towards change (the second curve). Strategic alliances are a good example of voluntary cooperation in which organizations combine resources to deal with the uncertainty created by environmental forces beyond their direct control (Gulati, 1999). Organizations enter into strategic alliances in order to share resources, such as personnel, finances, materials, and information. As strategic alliances belong to a kind of network, they have implications for wealth generation in terms of the perceived relationship value.

In addition, the resource interdependencies that exist among corporations can be examined in terms of alliance capitalism. The variety of the corporations involved and their network resources has a major effect on alliance capitalism in terms of new assets acquired via combining heterogeneous resources and utilization of scarce resources. It follows that the core competencies of a corporation are derived from the collective resources of other corporations in the network or network capabilities that would enhance national and international competitiveness of the corporation (Eng, 2007). Figure 3.3 presents a framework for developing strategic alliances. A corporation's leader needs to know that the impact of external factors results in an iterative series of sustainable change. Corporations must establish links with outside organizations and form a network when dealing with external impacts. Moreover, a corporation's strategic alliances form clusters that lead to inter-organizational resource sharing.

Clearly, Strategic alliances connect internal integration with market value (external integration) to capture new competitive advantage.

3.4 The development of a cluster

A cluster is a competitive strategy in which a number of corporations form an alliance for the purpose of sharing risk. Organizations use clustering to build strong ties with other organizations, serve as social institutions, earn social trust and build positive reputations, as well as to be included in social codebooks. Clustered corporations can also share information about trustworthiness, capabilities, and objectives (See Figure 3.3). Once a corporation finds that its competitiveness is declining, clusters can present opportunities for the organization to overcome the difficulty through utilization the role of gatekeeper and resource sharing.

A corporation's industrial cluster can be further developed into competitive advantage including traded interdependences and non-traded interdependences. Traded interdependences exist in the economic field, and include licensing, alliances, acquisitions, and technological expertise. Non-traded interdependences exist outside the economic field, and include customs, cultures, beliefs, and institutions (Tallman, Jenkins, & Pinch, 2004). These aspects of competitive advantage have been attributed to interaction. The resulting trust enables industrial clusters to develop a learned pattern of adaptation (Mathews, 2003; Niu, 2009). A clustered corporation's choice of governance mechanisms is subsequently affected by path dependencies across transactions (Bell, Tracey, & Heide, 2009). Cluster transactions involving new product development can be evaluated on the basis of either creativity or speed of development (Ganesan, Malter, & Rindfeisch, 2005). Both traded interdependences and non-traded interdependences are the key to promoting corporation growth and sustaining competitive advantage.

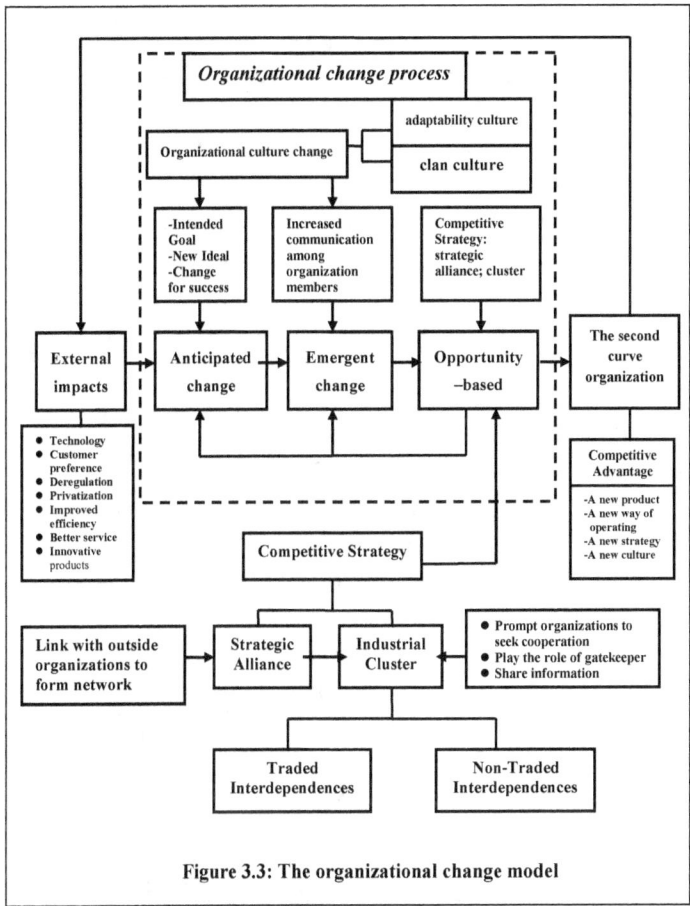

Figure 3.3: The organizational change model

Furthermore, clusters provide markets where commodities, services, and knowledge are traded in a highly efficient way among members without restricting their abilities to build pipelines and to interact with suppliers and customers located elsewhere. This market creates an environment that reduces the barriers to acquiring and utilizing the knowledge produced (Maskell & Lorenzen, 2004).

However, industrial clusters are not a panacea. Over time, the clustered corporations begin to experience resource diseconomies, isolated competitive practices, less frequent innovation, and lost dominance within the industry. Moreover, they will eventually become out-dated organizations or clusters, encountering great difficulties in the process. At this stage, the member organizations need to identify the problems and risks and activate the improvisational change model to assess the corporation's business status in which opportunity-based change will return to an anticipated change stage or an emergent change stage (See Figure 3.3). An organization in the change stage will revise its current strategy or offer a new competitive strategy to fulfill the requirements in the second curve.

This study sums up the development of organizational culture, the development of strategic alliance, and the development of a cluster in table 3.1. Table 3.1 presents the organizational change model, which has great capacity for the integration of internal and external resources. The change model is a feedback system that can reassess strategic direction and the development of new strategies to meet outside quickly change conditions. Such strategic changes necessitate the ongoing development of competent leaders and capable employees to integrate internal and external resources. Thanks to integrating internal and external resources, the change model enhances strategic partnerships and relationships.

Table3.1:The type of organizational integrating mechanism

Success dimensions	Organizational culture	Strategic alliance	Clusters
Internal integration	The clan culture focuses on participation, teamwork, and commitment towards the internal environment.	A corporation's strategic alliances form clusters that lead to inter-organizational resource sharing.	Traded interdependences exist in the economic field, and include licensing, alliances, acquisitions, and technological

			expertise.
External integration	The adaptability culture focuses on flexibility, creativity, innovation, and entrepreneurship towards the external environment.	Corporations must link with outside organizations and form a network in dealing with external impacts.	Non-traded interdependences exist outside the economic field, and include customs, cultures, beliefs, and institutions.

3.5 The development of organizational characteristics

Daft states, "Strategy is one important factor that affects organization design" (2007, p.63). This study adopts the strategic alliance and cluster strategy to create the second curve of organizational growth. In order to cope with strategy's change, an organization's characteristics need to change in accordance with the expected outcome of its strategy (see table 3.2). These organizational characteristics are highlighted in past literature reviews. These characteristics appear to promote aspects such as networking, flexibility and cooperation.

A strategic alliance can constitute a social network is based on openness, collaboration, teamwork, innovation, adaptation, flexibility, and responsiveness. Strategic alliance can embed among individual employees, influence their behavior, and extended to organization (Gulati, 1998). The organization combines heterogeneous resources and the utilization of scarce resources. A cluster strategy, on the other hand, requires the complementarity of the network, intense interpenetration, and an emphasis on entrepreneurial leadership towards the external environment. The cluster unions of organizations are flexible organization and cooperation culture that have common benefits and make certain the success of effort for corporation. The organization plays the role of a gatekeeper and there is sharing of information about trustworthiness, capabilities, and objectives.

Table 3.2: Organizational change along with strategies

Organizational change along with strategies	
Strategy: strategic alliance **Organization Characteristics:** • Openness, collaboration, teamwork, innovation; learned patterns of adaptation • Flexibility and responsiveness • Network of relationships • Combining heterogeneous resources and utilization of scarce resources	**Strategy:** cluster strategy **Organization Characteristics:** • The complementarity of the network ; intense interpenetration • The diversity of the network • An emphasis on Entrepreneurial leadership towards external environment • The development of a cooperation culture • Flexible organization • Share information regarding trustworthiness, capabilities, and objectives • Traded interdependences, and non-traded interdependences

3.6 Output goals

When organizations attain their goals (the second curve), the outputs (indicators) do not typically evaluate performance in terms of profitability, growth, market share, and return on investment. This model's output goals put emphasis on a corporation's competitive advantage, which may take the form of a new product, a new way of operations, a new strategy, and a new culture. They belong to qualitative indicators or so-called "soft" indicators, the evaluation of effectiveness based on characteristics emphasizing the actual output. This study defines these indicators present at table 3.3.

Table 3.3: Output indicator's definition

Output Indicator	Definition
A new product	A new product is the term used to describe the complete process of bringing a new product to market. It involves the idea generation, product design, and detail engineering.
A new way of operations	A new way of operations is to help organization or leaders rethink the use of process of operating for innovation.
A new strategy	A new strategy is for corporation's sustainable development and competitive advantage which has integrated internal common opinions and has created a new management strategy
A new culture	Outside influences, through a process known as cultural diffusion, may stimulate cultural change and form a new culture.

These outputs (indicators) lead the corporation toward another growth stage. In order for a corporation to stay competitive, it must continuously create the second curve. The quality indicator provides continuous feedback that is required for control. It is easy to monitor when the organizational change process is going out of control.

CHAPTER 4: CRITICAL EVALUATION

4.1 Method of Critical Evaluation
Five expert reviewers have examined the organizational change model presented in this study and offered constructive criticism. The reviewers include one general manager, one vice general manager, one CEO, one director of HR, and one department manager. (Additional background information is provided in Appendix A.) Each expert reviewer responded to the following evaluation items: (1) Contribution to the practice of management; (2) Originality of topic or approach; (3) Quality of references; (4) Validity of assumptions; (5) Rigor (theory, argument); (6) Thoroughness of presentation; (7) Validity of conclusions/propositions; (8) Writing quality (structure, logic, clarity); and (9) Overall comments (See Appendix B).

In item no. 1, which is the contribution to the practice of management. All of my expert reviewers agree with me that the topic contributes to the practice of management. They think "Timing" for organizational change is important to an enterprise and this dissertation can produce significant contributions, which would be of use in the real commercial world. Clusters and Strategic alliances are very popularly adopted tools for sustaining competitive advantage. Whereas one reviewer believes that the theory of clustering would be better suited to the manufacturing industry. Additionally, it could be applicable to a small proportion of service related industries.

In item no. 2, which is the originality of topic or approach. Some reviewers reflected positively on the concept, this study highlights possible approaches or methods, and timing in the light of ever-changing external environments as it can provide solutions to sustain competitive advantage in the transition. One such reviewer indicated that a specific research method should be clearly outlined.

In item no. 3, which is the quality of references. The

majority of the reviewers think the paper has appropriately highlighted the use of references to support its concept. However, one reviewer suggests that a period of references from the 1990s to end of 2009 will be more suitable.

In item no. 4, which is the validity of assumptions. All of the reviewers believe that the assumptions provided within this study are valid. However, one reviewer suggests that cultural differences between the East and West must be considered. Another reviewer suggests that more assumptions that are specific can be used to support the Cluster and Strategic Alliance theory and how they would impact upon the firm's performance and competitiveness, versus traditional approaches such as low-cost strategy that can't help organizations create platforms and opportunities for organizational success transition

In item no. 5, which is rigor (theory, argument). The majority of the reviewers think that this study is quite rigid. However, one expert reviewer's comments can be more detailed in interpreting how these theories can be applied to aid a company's transition, while other traditional methods such as low-cost strategy or differentiation do not have the advantages.

In item no. 6, which is the thoroughness of presentation. One of the expert reviewers suggests including to define the meaning of "while the firm is still successful" because most corporations are not capable of correctly performing self-evaluation.

In item no.7, which is the validity of conclusions/propositions. One reviewer appreciates that the presented ideas are good and that they could be very useful for some corporations seeking a breakthrough in business. However, some reviewers suggest that it is essential to consider culture difference. The conclusion will discuss the implementation of these suggestions in future studies.

In item no. 8, which is writing quality (structure, logic, clarity). The majority of expert reviewers think that the whole document is easy to read and understand. One evaluator suggests that definitions of some theories should be included within the "Introduction" or "Literature Review".

In item no. 9 which are the overall comments, one expert reviewer gave this study five suggestions as follows:

(1) The expert reviewer strongly suggests that we define the meaning of "successful" in order to form an alert system for the change model.

(2) The definition of "successful "should be related to the status of strategic alliance and cluster.

(3) Try to make the corporations change by "evolution" instead of "revolution" to ensure better acceptance and better implementation.

(4) In the real world, all changes are "on going" and take place on both a larger and faster scale. Hence, how to make a corporation aware of the real- time situation in order to take real-time action is critical. Timing is essential.

(5) All corporations are operated by people, so, cultural background plays an important role in organizational change. In strategic alliances and clusters, all parties are operated by people. The expert reviewer suggests that the cultural aspects should also be discussed in this study to ensure all major factors are taken into consideration.

4.2 Results of Critical Evaluation

The evaluations were provided by the five expert reviewers (see Appendix C), the study identified the following ten weaknesses in the light of above nine items that five expert reviewers have suggested:

(1) The theory of clustering is most applicable to the manufacturing industry, and may not be very applicable to service-related industries and corporations seeking organizational change to sustain competitiveness.

(2) The specific research method should be mentioned clearly.

(3) References from the 1990s onwards would be more suitable.

(4) More specific evidence is required to support how the

cluster and strategic alliance theory would affect a corporation's performance and competitiveness, against traditional approaches.

(5) There needs to be a more detailed analysis of how these theories can be applied to help a corporation's transition, in ways that traditional methods are incapable.

(6) Although the assumptions of this dissertation are valid, it would be better if it included an additional market survey from different industries to support its assumptions.

(7) Culture should also be discussed in this study to ensure that all major factors are considered in detail.

(8) The best way to enact change is evolution, not revolution, especially since subtle changes could result in faster success within the corporations.

(9) It is necessary to define the meaning of "while the firm is still successful," because most corporations are unsure about how to accurately evaluate their success.

(10) Some of the points are repetitive and definitions of some theories should be included in "Introduction" or "Literature Review".

This study was revised based on these comments. For example, the study has extended the references to include 2010, adopted some additional cases to compare the cluster and strategic alliance performance with that of traditional approaches, added organizational culture to the organizational change model, found over 18 articles indicating that organizational culture and strategy are highly interrelated, included some cases to interpret the differences between cluster theory and traditional methods, added the meaning of "successful" to the section titled "Implementing change in the successful stage", and input relevance to the field of theories in the "Introduction". The results of critical evaluation are as follows (see table 4.1):

Table 4.1: Comments and Responses Form

Comments	Responses
(1) The theory of clustering is most applicable to the manufacturing industry, and may not be very applicable to service-related industries and corporations seeking organizational change to sustain competitiveness.	According to Taiwan's National Central Library database, many researches have been conducted on cluster theory in such service-related industries as tourism and home-stays.
(2) The specific research method should be mentioned clearly.	This study guesses "the specific research method" is the improvisational change model. This study will interpret this method further.
(3) References from the 1990s onwards would be more suitable.	This study has extended the references to include 2010.
(4) More specific evidence is required to support how the cluster and strategic alliance theory would affect a firm's performance and competitiveness, versus traditional approaches.	This study accepts the suggestion and has adopted some additional cases to compare the cluster and strategic alliance performance with that of traditional approaches such as low-cost strategy.
(5) There needs to be a more detailed analysis of how these theories can	This study has included some cases to interpret the differences between cluster

be applied to help a corporation's transition, in ways traditional methods are incapable.	theory and traditional methods such as low-cost strategy.
(6) Although the assumptions of this study are valid, it would be better if it included an additional market survey from different industries to support its assumptions.	Yes, this will be done. In addition, this study suggests that this opinion can be studied in future research.
(7) Culture should also be discussed in this study to ensure that all major factors are well considered.	This study has added organizational culture to my conceptual model. In addition, this study has found 18 articles indicating that organizational culture and strategy are highly interrelated.
(8) The best way to enact change is evolution, not revolution, especially since subtle changes could result in faster success within the corporations.	This study's organizational change process is not revolution, but evolution.
(9) It is necessary to define the meaning of "while the corporation is still successful" because most corporations are	1. This study has added the meaning of "successful" to the section titled **"Implementing change in the successful stage"**.

unsure about how to evaluate correctly their success.	2. The organizational change model is an alert system because it has a feedback and check system.
(10) Some of the points are repetitive and definitions of some theories should be included in "Introduction" or "Literature Review".	This study has eliminated the repetitive points. Additionally, relevance to the field of theories has been included in the "Introduction".

CHAPTER 5: IMPLICATIONS

5.1 Implications for management

Organizational change process represents an organization's response to the presence of various stimulants, such as adaptation to environmental conditions, organizational decline, executive succession, and improvement in the corporation's effectiveness and performance (Santos & Garcia, 2006). This study has seven implications for management by conducting research. The seven implications of management have greatly contributed to corporations' transition toward competitive advantage (See Table 5.1). When corporations stumble upon a difficult position, the organizational change model can assist corporations to mitigate risk through the organizational change process. It is a loop system that has feedback and monitor functions. This study emphasizes organization's entrepreneurial spirits. Entrepreneurial spirits can influence corporation's decisions to initiate changes that are needed to adopt strategic alliances and clusters to connect with external environment to obtain new information and technology in order to remain competitive. However, inventions and technological developments in a society, such as the Internet or the automobile, can also have an impact on culture. Corporations must adjust organizational culture to adapt to external changes as well. In addition, this study's model can also assist corporations to create value-chain through improving activities, discover a new market space for a breakthrough in competitions, maintain long-term growth by continuously creating the second curve, and provide ISO 9000 and ISO 14000 standard functions. Relevance to the contribution of management is compiled in table 5.1 and analyzed individually as follows:

Table 5.1: Relevance to the contribution of management

Implications for management	Function and contribution
1. Loop system	Once the second curve begins to move downwards, the organization's leaders can start the loop to reduce risk and create a secondary curve.
2. Essential elements for successful transitions: culture, strategic alliances and clusters	Strategic alliances and clusters are essential elements for most successful transitions because they are the key to business cooperation, commercial information, and legislative advance.
3. Organization of entrepreneurial spirit	The organizational change model encourages entrepreneurial values, norms, and beliefs, because corporations in hypercompetitive environments need to become more entrepreneurial to adjust to emerging threats
4. Creating value-chain	The organizational change process has created a value-chain. That is to say, the value chain comes from the improvisational change model for diagnosing competitive advantage and forms the secondary curve. The value chain can also play a valuable role in organizational change.
5. Long-term growth	The organizational change model is a sustainability strategy model, since it maintains a corporation's growth in the long run.
6. Finding a new market space	The second curve is the new market space that can look across time from the value a market

	delivers today to the value it might deliver tomorrow. By thinking across conventional boundaries of competition, corporation can make strategic move that reconstructs established market space.
7. Providing the paths for translating strategies into realities	The organizational change model can provide the paths for translating strategies into realities, for the most part, the organizational change model has the following ISO 9000 and ISO 14000 standard functions: policy and management commitments; setting objectives and targets; planning; implementation; measurement, evaluation, and risk management; review and continuous improvement.

5.1.1 Loop system

The organizational change model makes use of a parallel development process to keep the first curve alive long enough for the second curve to firmly establish itself (Blanchard, 1996). A corporation must simultaneously meet two critical objectives: 1) perceiving external change and 2) building up a strategic intent for employees. This is a good way to sustain competitive advantage.

However, as the external environment is very dynamic, an organization has to deal with the fact that outside change does affect a corporation's competitive advantage. When an organization is in the successful stage, it has to create a new growth curve to maintain its competitive advantage. This study suggests that corporations can employ a competitive strategy (strategic alliance and cluster theory) to successfully achieve these objectives through the organizational change process. This competitive strategy can also assist an organization in achieving an organizational goal (the second curve). However, once the second curve begins to move downwards and the corporation begins to lose core competence, the organization's leaders need to start the loop (the improvisational change model) to check and solve the problems, and create a secondary curve.

The organizational change model is a loop system that has correction function to mitigate risk and update itself, and ensures that the organization can fast recover competitiveness after a disaster or a difficulty. The loop system also has a management review, which evaluates the performance of the organizational change model and execution of the organizational change process.

5.1.2 Essential elements for successful transitions: culture, strategic alliances and clusters

In addition, external clusters and customers, as well as internal employees, all play a role in determining a corporation's competitive strategy. All these changes require planning to overcome resistance to change, to find an idea that fits the need, to formulate a vision and strategy to meet the change, to continuously sustain a high degree of disciplined practice from the employee, and to create a new way of thinking. Furthermore, all above changes have to follow the organization's culture. An organization will not survive without a culture that supports openness, adaptability, employee participation, and ensuring a disciplined process.

However, the best opportunity for a successful transition is when an organization's members have a common objective of how to successfully implement the new strategy. Strategic alliances and clusters are essential elements for most successful transitions because they are the key to business cooperation, commercial information, and legislative advance. They are also tools used for common marketing, sharing of activities, resources, splitting of expenses, and thus of results (Enache et al., 2009). A strategic alliance can also take the form of a cluster through partnerships with suppliers, distributors, and also government agencies and universities.

The presence of clusters can transform cooperation and resources into a corporation's competitive advantage.

5.1.3 Organization of entrepreneurial spirit

The organizational change model encourages entrepreneurial values, norms, and beliefs, because corporations in hypercompetitive environments need to have more entrepreneurial spirit to adjust to emerging threats (Covin & Slevin, 1991). In addition, the use of the core organizational change model emphasizes developmental culture values and encourages internal entrepreneurial behavior by utilizing a competitive management strategy.

Jelinek & Littererstate state that entrepreneurial organizations "repeatedly initiate new product or service ideas... reconverting their people and assets to new users, bringing new ideas from many sources into good currency. Ideas must be generated, resources assembled, the new product or services produced and delivered to users by organization-wide redirection and cooperation" (1995, pp. 137-138). They also emphasize that an "organization must sustain such effort again and again" (1995, p. 138). Conversely, organizations with less dynamic entrepreneurial environments will result in performance decline (Ahuja & Lampert, 2001). That is to say, organizations act entrepreneurially in order to adapt to changing conditions and to seize opportunities.

5.1.4 Creating value-chain

The organizational change process has created a value-chain, from anticipated change to opportunity-based change. This has resulted in the formation of a relationship among upstream, midstream, and downstream resources. Every change's activity is value activity. Value activities are related by linkages that can lead to competitive advantage within the value chain. Porter states, "Linkages often reflect tradeoffs among activities to achieve the same overall result "(1985, p 48). In this study, the organizational change model can link among value activities to fill the value-chain. When activities in the value-chain are linked, changing is executed, and can achieve the second curve.

In addition, the organizational change model is a map that provides coordination for organization through internal and external sources in order to improve a corporation's ability to create a value chain and maintain a competitive advantage. The value chain comes from the improvisational change model for diagnosing competitive advantage and forms the second curve. The value chain, the organizational change process, can also play a coordination role in an organizational change.

5.1.5 Long-term growth

The organizational change model is oriented towards the second curve. The second curve represents new ideas and creativity, and starts by redefining the value-chain. Hence, the organizational change model can assist an organization to redefine the value-chain by keeping connections with outside organizations and finding the place in a corporation's value chain before someone else (Morrison, 1998). That is to say, corporation's long-term growth exists not only within corporation's value-chain, but between corporation's chain and outside organizations' value-chain.

A value-chain that is a source of growth can create the second curve and bring exponential market growth created by strategic alliance and industrial clusters. Once a corporation discovers the way to acquire a competitive advantage from the second curve, it will realize its growth in the long run. Therefore, the organizational change model is a sustainable strategy model, since it maintains a corporation's growth in the long run.

5.1.6 Finding a new market space

The organizational change model is the path or process to find a new market space and applies strategic alliance and industrial clusters to focus on the new market space. The second curve is the new market space that is a corporation's relative performance across its industry's factors of competition. Actually, a corporation would prefer to create a new market space, it has to reconstruct market break from the competition. Moreover, the new market space can "look across time from the value a market delivers today to the value it might deliver tomorrow"(Kim & Mauborgne, 2005, p.75). That is to say, the new market space is a continuously creative market.

How does a corporation conceive a new market space? By thinking across the organizational change model, corporation can see how to make convention-altering, strategic moves that reconstruct established market space. For example, Cisco System created a new market space by thinking across time trends of the growing demands for high–speed data exchanges. In addition, based on the rising tide of globalization, CNN created the first twenty-four-hour global news network. Corporation keeps its sights on the evolving mass market and not to fall into competitive benchmarking (Kim & Mauborgne, 2005). The ultimate of the corporation will get a new value and keep its sustainable business development.

5.1.7 Providing the paths for translating strategies into realities

The organizational change model can provide the paths or guideline for translating strategies into realities, for the most part, the organizational change model has the following ISO 9000 and ISO 14000 standard functions: (1) policy and management commitments;(2) setting objectives and targets;(3)planning; (4)implementation;(5)measurement, evaluation, and risk management;(6) review and continuous improvement.

Also, the organizational change model can integrate the external resources of organization and internal resources of organization into the second curve on account of owning those standard functions.

5.2 Limitations and Future implications for research
5.2.1 Limitations

5.2.1.1 Leaders mindset

The main limitation of the organizational change model is that if a corporation's leader does not want to change, then the organizational change model will not be very effective. Therefore, we must suppose that organization's leaders desire change in order to secure a competitive advantage. For the leader, change (the second curve) requires the daring and confidence because there are many tough things to cope with. For example, you must deal with the second curve and the first curve for them to simultaneously work at the same time. For the leader and employee, the second curve is a big change that is a little daunting because nobody knows if the second curve will results in redundancy.

5.2.1.2 Needing a just in time crisis-control system

In addition, since the Internet has a great impact on organizational communication, the organizational change model is unable to cope with certain situations. For example, if a corporation experiences constraints, the news will spread fast. Although the organizational change model owns the loop system, the loop system does not have a just-in-time crisis-control system because of lacking block and intercept function.

5.2.1.3 Corporation culture's static

A corporation culture supports the open exchange of ideas and views, empowers people to take part in corporation's change without conflict, resistance, or turmoil. While corporation culture is static, it is narrow and self-centered. It concentrates on making everlasting the existing strengths of the corporation rather than improving the capabilities of the whole corporation. The change model does not discuss corporation culture that must regard change as the norm, and does not discuss how to form a new culture of corporation to deal with corporation culture's static.

5.2.1.4 Assessment system lacks scientific research

Corporation that adopts the organizational change model

as its guiding business model must be adaptive and embrace change or focus on continuing improvement and ongoing change. However, change is difficult because it brings many uncertainties about future. Transforming a corporation into a more capable organization requires new ways of thinking and management, such as life cycle thinking (LCT) or life cycle management (LCM) (Rainey, 2006). "Management must assess the needs for change, defining what has to be improved, and how it is to be improved" (Rainey, 2006, p.513). Although this organizational change model has a loop system that can renew or rebuild new ways to overcome difficulty, the assessment system lacks scientific research to prove this change model's value.

5.2.2 Future research
5.2.2.1 Risk management

Change is everywhere throughout the risk function. When the first curve transfers to the second curve, we don't know what is going to happen. This study does not probe into risk management that develops corporation's programs and strategies to deal with risks that hedge traditional alternatives. Hence, future work on organizational change model can design a risk management system that includes impact (disaster tolerance), mitigation risk methods (precaution), and recovery.

The risk management system must be a secure operation or activity that ensures external change does not impact organization for the maintaining organizational competitiveness. Therefore, the risk management system must also be certifed periodically that security practices remain aligned correctly with outside change.

On the other hand, the risk management system is able to maintain the outcome of the output, such as a new product or a new way of operation. Thus the risk management system of future research must keep updating between threats and countermeasures to mitigate organization's risk.

5.2.2.2 Overcome governance problems

Many successful clusters are dominated by hierarchical patterns of interorganizational governance involving unilateral rules and standard operating procedures that originate from a predominant corporation (Markusen, 1996). This raises serious questions regarding the utility of current cluster theory in these contexts (Bell, Tracey & Heide, 2009). This study cannot overcome governance problems at present, and this is an area that requires in-depth research.

With respect to governance problems, apart from a predominant corporation, government incorrect regional policy also causes serious clusters questions and corporations' development. Future research on incorrect regional policy to corporation's influence can be further dicussed.

5.2.2.3 Put it into proper practice

Furthermore, the study makes use of the organizational change model to help corporation resolve internal and external factors' influence through competitive strategy. This change model can bring some new ideas (concepts) to corporations and can help them to deal with problems. However, if the corporation's leader doesn't put the change model into proper practice to cope with its problems or create new way for organization, this organizational change model will be still a general model that cannot effectively deal with corporation's difficulty position. This viewpoint is similar to one of the experts suggests, "Although the assumptions of this study are valid, it would be better if it included an additional market survey from different industries to support its assumptions." Hence, future work on organizational change model includes surveying the conditions of those successful corporations in ten years, such as Microsoft, Apply Inc., and TSMC, etc., and to prove and find their factors of success are engaged in their organizational change during the growth period.

In addition, this study suggests that future research can adopt the Grounded Theory to analyze or certify the organizational change model's practicality when mass quantitative information about those corporations' change during the growth period in our time is a problem. Grounded Theory aims to find data's concepts and relationships by interviews and observations to organize theoretical explanatory scheme, it perhaps resolves those problems that lacks mass quantitative information.

5.2.2.4 Establish LCA system

The organizational change model provides a graphic representation of the key elements or processes for corporation change. The change model takes a cradle-to-grave view, but it does not provide a LCA (life cycle assessment). LCA examines and analyzes all of the inputs and outputs, their consequences and influences, problems and solutions through using exact quantitative and qualitative analyses. LCA can assist improved strategic positions and moderated negative influences, and be able to probe the possibilities for systemic improvements through new product design, and deployment (Graedel, 1998; Rainey, 2006). In the future research, we can establish LCA or develop a quality measure to evaluate the organizational change model. These steps can include key goals, metrics, performance, development, and improvement.

In addition, according to organizational goals or the second curve, corporation's leader can decide the scope of the LCA and gives the LCA framework. The LCA framework can be a repeating process in order to achieve full understanding. Rainey (2006) suggested frameworks for LCA based on time and complexity because "time relates to the life of the product and the duration of satisfaction that solution provide" (p.566). Thus, by applying the organization change model, the LCA framework of the future research is very useful for understanding opportunities to improve processes, enhance the linkages and communications between the organization and outside organization.

APPENDIX A: THE EXPERT REVIEWERS

Although David Tsai and James Chueh do not have a theoretical background in this dissertation topic, they have extensive experience in the field. The other reviewers have strong theoretical backgrounds and extensive working experience in the dissertation topic. With respect to their professional title and their companies, please see the list below.

Number	Name	Professional Title	Company	Reference
1	David Tsai	Deputy General Manager	Far EasTone Telecommunication Co., Ltd.	
2	Simon Hsieh	CEO	Yougic Biotech Co., Ltd.	
3	Walter Huang	Director, HR Div.	INNOLUX Display Corp.	
4	Andy Liu	Vice Chairman, President and CEO	MCSI, eGlobal Management Corp.	Backup Reviewers
5	James Chueh	Department Manager, Wireless Product Div.	ZyXEL Communications Corp.	Backup Reviewers

APPENDIX B: EVALUATION FORM

Please rate each of the following items on a scale of 1 to 5, with 1 being low, and 5 being high. In addition, please write a brief comment for each item.

Items	Rating	Comments
1. Contribution to the practice of management		
2. Originality of topic or approach		
3. Quality of the references		
4. Validity of assumptions		
5. Rigor (theory, argument)		
6. Thoroughness of presentation		
7. Validity of conclusions/propositions		

APPENDIX C: INTEGRATED EVALUATION FORM

Please rate each of the following items on a scale of 1 to 5, with 1 being low, and 5 being high. In addition, please write a brief comment for each item.

Items	Expert Reviewer	Rating	Comments
1. Contribution to the practice of management	CEO Hsieh	4	The points that were raised are valid in order to improve organizational change.
	Director Huang	4	"Timing" for organization change is important to an enterprise. With this paper, any one from an enterprise who cares about competitive advantages for his/her enterprise should pay more attention to organization development to face the change.
	President, CEO Liu	3	The theory of clustering would

			work mostly in manufacturing industry; it may not be that much applicable to service related industries and firms seeking for organizational changes to sustain company competitiveness.
	Vice General Manager Tsai	5	1. As I worked in wireless telecommunication Industry Company in Taiwan, due to deregulation and loosened government policies, telecommunication industry business environments is also moving

| | | | towards liberation and have greater competitions. We are always looking for strategic alliances opportunities to sustain our market leadership position and maximize shareholders value. 2. This dissertation can function properly and will be very useful in the real commercial world. Clusters and Strategic alliances are very |

| | | | | popularly adopted tools for sustaining competitive advantage. In addition, this concept paper clearly provides solutions for a company to maintain its competitiveness, including organizational change, the organizational life cycle and the improvisational change model, etc. In addition, it shows the best timing for a company to change is when it is still in successful stage, which |

			refers to the second curve. 3. Normally, Firms miss the best critical timing ("S-shaped") to change and improvisational change model. 4. I learn a lot from this dissertation and will apply this to the firm, if I have opportunities to run a business in the future.
	Manager Chueh	4	From my perspective, it is more important for organization to change according to its positioning, i.e., technical

			provider or product, service provider. However, the positioning shall align with external factor, i.e., supply chain and industrial ecosystem. This type of research is quite valuable for a company like us to manage change.
2. Originality of topic or approach	CEO Hsieh	4	Very creative and meaningful. Strategic alliance and cluster do make changes.
	Director Huang	4	The originality & motivation are great. Suggestion: Specific research method should be mentioned clearly.
	President Liu	4	The concept paper points out

			possible approaches and timing, in light of ever-changing external environment.
	Vice General Manager Tsai	4	It takes the overall situation of the firm into consideration and provides solutions to sustain a competitive advantage in the transition.
	Manager Chueh	4	This viewpoint is new for me.
3. Quality of references	CEO Hsieh	5	Very good
	Director Huang	4	Time frame of references from 1990s to end of 2009 will be more suitable.
	President Liu	4	The paper has appropriately highlighted the use of references to support its concept

UPDATED

	Vice General Manager Tsai	5	Over 50 references are quoted and taken into this dissertation and it covers organization and management theories of the past 20 years.
	Manager Chueh	5	It is clear and complete.
4. Validity of assumptions	CEO Hsieh	4	Quite practical and close to genuine situation.
	Director Huang	4	Direction is ok. Suggestion: Cultural differences such as Western V.S. Eastern, capitalism V.S. socialism could be mentioned.
	President Liu	3	Assumptions that are more specific can be used to support the Cluster and Strategic Alliance

			theory and how they would impact the firm's performance and competitiveness, versus traditional approaches.
	Vice General Manager Tsai	4	The assumptions on this dissertation are valid. It would be better if there were additional market survey from different industries to support its assumptions.
	Manager Chueh	5	The assumption of firms' life cycle is definitely correct.
5. Rigor (theory, argument)	CEO Hsieh	4	The best way to create change is through evolution, not revolution, especially in reality silent change brings rapid success to

UPDATED

			the firm.
	Director Huang	4	No comment
	President Liu	3	Can be more detailed in interpreting how these theories are applied to help a company's transition; Why other traditional methods do not have the advantages.
	Vice General Manager Tsai	4	As a Vice President of a wireless Company in Taiwan, In my point of view, this dissertation is quite rigid.
	Manager Chueh	4	I do not know much about this but it looks rigid.
6. Thoroughness of presentation	CEO Hsieh	4	Suggest to add the definition "the firm is still successful" because most

81

			firms are unsure when it comes to self-evaluation.
	Director Huang	4	No comment
	President Liu	3	Some of the points are repetitive.
	Vice General Manager Tsai	5	The presentation is excellent in this dissertation; the framework, sequence and conclusions are very good.
	Manager Chueh	4	The presentation is quite clear.
7. Validity of conclusions/pr opositions	CEO Hsieh	4	Culture difference.
	Director Huang	4	Conclusion brings out your suggestion about " further studies "
	President Liu	4	The ideas are good and could be very useful for some firms seeking business

UPDATED

			breakthrough.
	Vice General Manager Tsai	5	The conclusions in this dissertation are valid and workable. The way to execute them and the way to control timing would be challenging.
	Manager Chueh	4	I believe it is helpful for firm transition.
8. **Writing quality (structure, logic, clarity)**	CEO Hsieh	4	Pretty good in writing quality.
	Director Huang	4	Definitions of some theories should be put in "Introduction" or "Literature Review".
	President Liu	4	Generally, a piece of well written "concept" document
	Vice General Manager	4	I am not qualified to give a rating in this

	Tsai		item because my writing ability is not very good.
	Manager Chueh	5	The whole document is easy to read and understandable.
9. Overall comments	CEO Hsieh		1. I strongly suggest we should define the meaning of "successful" in order to form an alert system to the change model. 2. The definition of "successful "should be related to the status of strategic alliance and cluster. 3. Try to make the firms change by "evolution" instead of "revolution"

			to ensure better acceptance and better implementation.

4. In real world, all changes are "on going" and now it is changing faster in bigger scale. Hence, how to make a firm aware of the real-time situation to take real-time action is very critical. Timing is essential.
5. All corporations are operated by people, so, culture background plays an important role

			in organizational change. In strategic alliance and cluster, all parties are operated by people. I suggest that culture aspect should also be discussed in this paper to ensure all major factors are taken into consideration.

ENDNOTE

Warrian & Mulhern (2009) synthesize the research findings on innovation and learning in four industrial clusters in advanced manufacturing and mining sectors: the automotive steel clusters in Hamilton, the automotive parts clusters in Windsor, the aerospace clusters in Montreal, and the mining supply and services cluster in Sudbury. These four industrial clusters faced both internal and external constraints on their further development and innovation, stemming from their gestation within the previous era of industrial production. Moreover, they also faced global market competition pressure. Hence, they must change their structure through vertical supply chain and internalize R&D by adopting a clustered pattern of industrial organization, characterized by a regional concentration of networked suppliers, inter-firm learning, and a decentralized and flattened production chain. In addition, they are facing the ongoing reorganization of the global supply chain, which generates additional pressure to increase productivity and reduce costs in order to maintain relationships with assemblers and manufacturers. Once they faced the challenge of making the transition from one form of industrial production to another, firms tend to avoid traditional manufacturing and resource industries. However, the question of whether or not the common denominators of successful adaptation can apply to other sectors requires further data collection and analysis.

REFERENCES

Ahuja, G. & Lampert,C. M. (2001). Entrepreneurship in the large corporation: A longitudinal study of how established firms create breakthrough innovations. *Strategic Management Journal*, 22, 521-543.

Allen, R. S. & Montgomery, K. A. (2001). Applying an organizational development approach to creating diversity. *Organizational dynamics*, 30 (2), 149-161.

Andersen, T. K., Buvik, M. P, & Torvatn, H. (2007). Developing criteria for healthy organization change. *Work & Stress*, 21(3), 243-263.

Andrews, K. (1971). *The Concept of Corporate Strategy*. Dow Jones-Irwin: Homewood, IL.

Andrus, J. F. (2004). Electric AMR market enters its second curve — Autovation. *Utility Automation & Engineering T&D*, 9 (4), 24-26.

Athiyaman, A. & Parkan, C. (2008). A functionalist framework for identifying business clusters: Applications in Far North Queensland. *Australian Journal of Management*, 33(1), 202-229.

Barkema, H. G. (2008). Toward unlocking the full potential of acquisitions the role of organizational restructuring. *Academy of Management Journal*, 51 (4).696-722.

Bell, S. J., Tracey, P. & Heide, J. B. (2009). The organization of regional clusters. *Academy of Management Review*, 34 (4), 623-642.

Blanchard, K. (1996). Becoming a world class organization. *Executive Edge Newsletter*, 27 (10), 2-3.

Bonham, N. A. (2003). ISO: A Quality Management System: increase efficiency and the bottom line. *Alaska Business Monthly*, 19 (10). 123-128.

Brown, A. D. & Starkey, K. (1994). The effect of organizational culture on communication and information. *Journal of Management Studies*, 31 (6), 807-828.

Bruton, G. D., Ahlstrom, David., Li, Han-Lin. (2010). Institutional Theory and entrepreneurship: where are we now and where do we need to move in the future? Entrepreneurship: Theory & Practice, 34 (3), 421-440.

Cameron, K. S. &Freeman, S. J. (1991). Cultural congruence, strength, and type: relationships to effectiveness. *Research in Organizational Change and Development*, 5, 23-58.

Chatman J. A. & Cha, S. E. (2003). Leading by leveraging culture. *California Management Review*, 45 (4), 20-34.

Chamberlin, J. (2010). Business process reengineering. *Management Service*, 54 (1), 13-20.

Christensen, C. M. (1992). Exploring the limits of the technology S-curve. *Production and Operations Management Journal*, 1, 334-366.

Chong, A. Yee-Loong, Ooi, Keng-Boon, Lin, B. & Teh, Pei-Lee. (2010). TQM, knowledge management and collaborative commerce adoption: A literature review and research framework. *Total Quality Management*,

21 (5), 457-473.

Churchill, N. C. & Lewis, V. L. (1983). The five stages of small business growth, *Harvard Business Review*, 61, 30-50.

Collins, P., Hage, J. & Hull,F. (1998). Organizational and technological predictors of change in automaticity, *Academy of Management Journal*, 31, 512-43.

Cowan, R. & Jonard, N. (2009). Knowledge portfolios and the organization of innovation networks. *Academy of Management Review*, 34(2), 320-342.

Covin, J. G. & Slevin, D. P. (1991). A conceptual model of entrepreneurship as firm behavior. *Entrepreneurship Theory and Practice*, 16, 7-25.

Daft, R. L. (2007). *Organization Theory and Design*. Thomson South-Western:USA.

Damson, M. (2009). New regions and regionalisation through clusters – city-regions and new problems for the periphery. *International Journal of Public Sector Management*, 22 (3), 260-271.

Denison, D. R. & Mishra, A. K. (1995). Toward a theory of organizational culture and effectiveness. *Organization Science*, 6 (2), 204-223.

Dewitt, T., Giunipero, L. C. & Melton, H. L. (2006). Clusters and supply chain management: the Amish experience. *International Journal of Physical Distribution & Logistics Management*, 36(4), 289-308.

Dixon, M. A. (2010). Managing the multiple meaning of organizational culture in interdisciplinary collaboration and consulting. *Journal of Business Communication*, 47 (1), 3-19.

Eisenberg, E. & Riley, P. (2000). *Organizational culture*. In Jablin & Putnam (Eds.), The new handbook of organizational communication: Advances in theory, research, and methods, a thousand, CA: Sage, 291-317.

Enache, E., Vechiu, C. & Morozan, C. (2009). The cluster association—a form of business development. *Theoretical & Applied Economics*, 37-44.

Eng, T. Y. (2007). Relationship value of firms in alliance capitalism and implications for FDI. *International Journal of Business Studies,* 15(1), 43-68.

Ettlie, J. E., Bridges, W.P. & O'Keefe, R. D. (1984). Organizational strategy and structural differences for radical versus incremental innovation. *Management Science*, 30, 682-698.

Ettlie, J. E. (1992). Organizational integration and process innovation. *Academy of Management Journal*, 35 (4), 795-827.

Farina, E. M. Q. & Zylbersztajn, D. (2003). Economics of networks and patterns of competition in food and agribusiness. Working Paper No. 3/027, University of Sao Paolo, Available at http://www.ead.fea.usp.br/Wpapers/63200714509.pdf. Accessed on October 30 2009.

Frahm, J. (2007). Organizational change; approaching the frontier, some faster than others. *Organization Review*, 14(6), 945-955.

Ganesan, S., Malter, A. J., & Rindfeisch, A. (2005). Does distance still matter? Geographic proximity in new product development. *Journal of Marketing*, 69 (4), 44-60.

Gharajedaghi, J. (2007). Systems thinking: a case for second-order-learning. *The Learning Organization*, 14(6). 473-479.

Ghobadian, A. & O'Regan, N. (2002). The link between culture, strategy, and performance in manufacturing SMEs. *Journal of General Management*, 28 (1). 16-34.

Giuliani, E. (2009). Cluster absorptive capacity: why do some clusters forge ahead and others lad behind? *European Urban and Regional Studies*, 12(3), 269-288.

Goodman, P. S. & Rousseau, D. M. (2004). Organizational change that produces results: the linkage approach. Academy of Management Executive, 18 (3), 7-19.

Grace, C., Hadyn, I. (2004). A new approach to benchmarking learning and development strategy. *International Journal of Contemporary Hospitality Management*, 16 (1), 52-58.

Graedel, T. E. (1998). *Streamlined life-cycle assessment.* Englewood Cliffs, NJ: Prentice Hall.

Gulati, R. (1998). Alliances and networks. *Strategic Management Journal*, 19, 293-317.

-----------. (1999). Where do interorganizational networks come from? *America Journal of Sociology*, 104(5), 1439-1493.

-----------. (1999). Network location and learning: the

influence of network resources and firm capabilities on alliance formation. *Strategic Management Journal*, 20, 397-420.

Gupta, V. & Subramanian, R. (2008). Seven perspectives on regional clusters and the case of Grand Rapids office furniture city. *International Business Review*, 17, 371-384.

Gwee, J. (2009). Innovation and the creative industries cluster: A case study of Singapore's creative industries. Innovation: *Management, Policy & Practice*, 11(2), 240-252.

Hage, J. T. (1999). Organizational innovation and organizational change. *Annual Review Social*, 25, 597-622.

Hervas-Oliver, J. L. & Albors-Garrigos, J. (2009). The role of the firm's internal and relational capabilities in clusters: when distance and embeddedness are not enough to explain innovation. *Journal of Economic Geography* 9, 263-283.

Higgins, J M. & Mcallaster, C. (2002). Want innovation? Then use cultural artifacts that support it. *Organizational Dynamics*, 31(1), 74-84.

Hill, C. W. L. (1992). Strategies for exploiting technological innovations: when and when not to license. *Organization Science*, 3, 428-441.

Hitt, M. A. (2000). The new frontier: Transformation of management for the new millennium. *Organizational Dynamics*, 28, 7-17.

Hooijberg, R. & Petrock, F. (1993). On cultural change: using the competing values framework to help leaders execute a transformational strategy. *Human Resource Management*, 32, 29-50.

Hospers, G. J. (2005). Best practices and the dilemma of regional cluster policy in Europe. *Tijdschrift Sociale en Eonomische Geografie, Outlook on Europe*, 96 (4), 452-457.

Ireland, D. R., Hitt, M. A., & Sirmon, D. G. (2003). A model of strategic entrepreneurship: The construct and its dimension. Journal of Management, 29, 963-989.

Jacobs, D. & Lankhuizen, M. (2006). De Nederlandse exportsterkte geclusterd. *Economisch Statisti,sche Berichten*, 91 (4487), 247-249.

Jelinek, M. & Litterer, J. (1995). Toward entrepreneurial organizations: Meeting ambiguity with engagement. *Entrepreneurship Theory and Practice*, 19 (3), 137-169.

Jokipii, A. (2010). Determinants and consequences of internal control in firms: a contingency theory based analysis. *Journal of Management & Governance*, 14 (2), 115-144.

Kim, W. C. & Mauborgne, R. (2005). Blue Ocean Strategy-How to create uncontested market space and make the competition irrelevant. US: Harvard Business School Publishing Corporation.

Khan, J. H. & Ghani, J. A. (2004). Clusters and entrepreneurship: implications for innovation in a developing economy. *Journal of Developmental Eentrepreneurship*, 9(3), 221-238.

Kuchinsakas, V. & Paulauskaite, N. (2005). Organization culture and its development in private colledges. *Quality of Higher Eduation*, 2, 144-165.

Kodama, M. (2005). Innovating business strategies through strategic communities-DocoMo's use of external expertise in the development of 3G technology. Sreategic Direction, 21 (10),9-11.

Kotter, J. P. & Heskett, J. L. (1992). *Corporate Culture and Performance*, New York: Free Press.

Kraats, M. & Zajac, E. (2001). How organizational resources affect strategic change and performance, turbulent environments: theory and evidence. *Organization Science,* 12, 632-657.

Lorenzen, M. (2002). Ties, trust, and trade—Elements of a theory of coordination in industrial clusters. Int. studies of management & organization, 31(4), 14-34.

Markusen, A. (1996). Sticky places in slippery spaces: A typology of industrial districts. *Economic Geography*, 72(3), 293-313.

Maskell, P. (2001). Towards a knowledge-based theory of the geographic cluster. *Industrial and Corporate Change*, 10(4), 921-943.

Maskell, P. & Lorenzen, M. (2004). The cluster as market organization. *Urban Studies*, 41(5/6), 991-1009.

Matopoulos, A., Vlachopoulou, M. & Manthou, V. (2006). Exploring chain, network and cluster collaborative practices: implications for SMEs. *Int, J. Networking and Virtual Organizations*, 3(2), 142-155.

Mathews, J. (2003). Competitive dynamics and economic learning: An extended resource-based view. *Industrial and Corporate Change*, 12(1), 115-145.

McDermott, C. M. & Stock, G. N. (1999). Organizational culture and advanced manufacturing technology implementation. Journal of Operations Management, 17, 521-533.

Miles, R. E., Snow, C. C., Meyer, A. D. & Coleman, H.J. (1978). Organizational strategy, structure, and process, Academy of Management Review, 3, 546-562.

Miller, D. & Friesen, P. H. (1984). A longitudinal study of the corporate life cycle, Management Science, 30, 1161-1183.

Morrison, J, I. (1998). The second curve: managing the velocity of change. *Strategy & Leadership January/February*, 6-11.

Mukherjee, A. S. (2009). Leading the networked organization. *Leader to Leader*, 23-29.

Neal, A. (2009). Preparing the organization for change. *Strategic HR Review*, 7(6), 30-35.

Nelson, R. & Winter, S. (1982). The schumpeterial tradeoff revisited. *American Economic Review*, 72, 114-133.

Niu, K. H. (2009). The involvement of firms in industrial clusters: A conceptual analysis. *International Journal of Management*, 26 (3), 445-455.

Orlikowski, W. J. & Hofman, J. D. (1997). An improvisational model for change management: The case of groupware technologies. *Sloan Management Review*/Winter, 11-21.

Orlikowski, W. J. (1996). Improvising organizational transformation over time: A situated change perspective. *Information Systems Research*, 7, 63-92.

Phillips, P. (2010). Culture and strategic leadership, *Business Corner-Strategies & Analysis*, 24-25.

Pickernell, D., Rowe, P. A., Christie, M. J. & Brooks bank, D. (2007). Developing a framework for network and cluster identification for use in economic development policy-making. *Entrepreneurship & Regional Development*, 19, 339-358.

Pietersen, W. (2002). The Mark Twain Dilemma: The theory and practice of change leadership. *Journal of Business Strategy*, 32-37.

Porter, B. L. & Parker, W. S. (1992). Culture change. *Human Resource Management*, 31, 45-67.

Porter, M. E. (1985). *Competitive advantage: creating and sustaining superior performance*. New York: Free Press.

---------------. (1998). Clusters and the new economics of competition. *Harvard Business Review*, 76(6), 77-90.

---------------. (1990). *The competitive advantage of nations*. Hound mills, The Macmillan Press.

---------------. (2001). *Cluster innovation: regional foundations of U.S. competitiveness*. Council of competitiveness, Washington, D. C.

Pouder, R. & ST. John, C. H. (1996). Hot spots and blind spots: geographical clusters of firms and innovation. *Academy of Management Review*, 21(4), 1192-1225.

Pouzar, E. (1996). RMS approaching second curve. *Property & Casualty Risk & Benefits Management*, 100 (43), 25.

Prajogo, D. I. & McDermott, D. M. (2005). The relationship between total quality management practices and organizational culture. International Journal of Operations & Production Management, 25 (11), 1101-1122.

Recardo, R., Molloy, K. & Pellegrino, J. (!995/96). How the learning organization manages change. *National Productivity Review*, 7-13.

Rainey, D. L. (2006). *Sustainable business development: inventing the future through strategy, innovation, and leadership*. New York: Cambridge University Press.

Santos, M. V., & Garcia, M. T. (2006). Organizational change: the role of managers' mental models. *Journal of Change Management*, 6 (3), 305-320.

Schein, E. H. (1990). Organizational culture. *American Psychologist*, 45, 109-119.

---------------. (1992). *Organizational Culture and Leadership*, 2d ed, Homewood, Ill: Richard D. Irwin.

---------------. (1985). *Organizational Culture and Leadership: A Dynamic View*, San Francisco: Jossey-Bass Publishers, CA.

Schilling, M. A. & Hill, C. W. L. (1998). Managing the new product development process: strategic imperatives. *Academy of Management Execuyive*, 12 (3), 67-81.

Senge, P. M. (1994). *The Fifth Discipline: The Art and Practice of the Learning Organization*. NewYork: Currency and Doubleday.

Shepherd, D. A., Patzelt, H., & Haynie, J. M. (2010). Entrepreneurial spirals: deviation-amplifying loops of an entrepreneurial mindset and organizational culyure, *Entrepreneurship Theory and Practice*, 59-82.

Sterman, J. D. (2000). *Systems Thinking and Modeling for a Complex World*. United States: The McGraw-Hill Companies.

Suarez, F. F. & Oliva R. (2005). Environmental change and organizational transformation. *Industrial and Corporate Change*, 14(6), 1017-1041.

Tallman, S., Jenkins, M., Henry, N., & Pinch, S. (2004). Knowledge, clusters, and competitive advantage. *Academy Management Review*, 29(2), 258-271.

Tseng, C. C. & Shih, C. C. (2008). Industrial cluster innovation: The case of Koji pottery. *Journal of Entrepreneurship Research*, 3(4), 25-37.

Toor, Shamas-ur-Rehman & Ofori, G. (2009). Ethical leadership: examining the relationships with full range leadership model, employee outcomes, and organizational culture. *Joural of Business Ethics*, 90, 533-547.

Treacy, M. & Wiersema, F. (1995). How market leaders

keep their edge. *Fortune*, 6, 88-98.

Utterback, J. & Suarez, F. (1993). Technology, competition and industry structure, *Research Policy*, 22, 1-21.

Visser, E. J. & Atzema, O. (2008). With or without clusters: facilitating innovation through a differentiated and combined network approach. European Planning Studies, 16 (9), 1169-1188.

Warner Burke, W. (2000). The new agebda for organizational development. *Organization Development and Transformation: Managing Effective Change*, Burr Ridge, Ill.: Irwin McGraw-Hill, 523-535.

Warrian, P. & Mulhern, C. (2009). From metal bashing to materials science and services: Advanced manufacturing and mining clusters in transition. European Planning Studies, 17(2), 281-301

Weigl, T., Hartmann, E., Johns, C. & Darkow, I. L (2008). Inter-organizational network structures in Russia: organizational changes from institutional and social embeddedness perspectives. *Human Resource Development International*, 11(2), 151-165.

Weigl, T., Hartmann, E., Jahns,C. & Darkow,I. L (2008). Inter-organizational network structures in Russia: organizational changes from institutional and social embeddedness perspectives. *Human Resource Development International*, 11(2), 151-165.

West, D. M. (2004). E-Government and the transformation of service delivery and citizen attitudes. Public

Administration Review, 64, 15-27.

Whelan-Berry, K. S. & Gordon, J. R. (2000). Effective organization change: new insights from multi-level analysis of the organizational change process. *Academy of Management Proceedings*, ODC: D1-D6.

Wintzberg, H. & Westley, F. (1992). Cycles of organizational change. *Strategic Management Journal*, 13, 39-59.

Wines, W. A. (2008). Seven pillars of business ethics: toward a comprehensive framework. *Journal of Business Ethics*, 79, 483-499.

Yeo, R. K. (2009). Electronic government as a strategic intervention in organizational change process. *Journal of Change Management*, 9 (3), 271-304.

Zhou, C. & Li, J. (2008). Product innovation in emerging market-based international joint ventures: An organizational ecology perspective. *Journal of International Business Studies*, 39 (7), 1114-1119.

Zu, X., Robbins, T. & Fredendall, L. D. (2010). Mapping the critical links between organizational culture and TQM/Six sugma practices. *Int. J. Production Economics*, 123, 86-106.

ABOUT THE AUTHOR

Dr. Spencer hsieh graduated from University of Maryland University College, USA. He has worked in government departments, business departments, and academic research units in Taiwan.

In the business field, he worked as a senior manager in the financial department and chairman of the board of LICO Technology Corp. Sometimes he also teaches at the Department of Marketing and Logistics of China University of Technology in Taiwan.

www.ingramcontent.com/pod-product-compliance
Lightning Source LLC
Chambersburg PA
CBHW052331220526
45472CB00001B/366